HOW TO MAKE NEWS & INFLUENCE PEOPLE

Dedication

This book is dedicated to the frustrated publicity chairman who wrote—

Dear Editor:

Whenever I send you a news story about the PTA you get it all wrong. Either a whole line is out of place so it doesn't make sense or your typesetter misspells the same words in the printed story that my typewriter misspelled in the copy. Doesn't he know how to spell? Hasn't he got a dictionary?

Anyway. I've figured out what to do. After this. when I send you a story about the PTA. please don't print it.

Sincerely.

Publicity Chairman

HOW TO MAKE NEWS
& INFLUENCE PEOPLE
By Morgan Harris & Patti Karp

TAB BOOKS
Blue Ridge Summit, Pa. 17214

FIRST EDITION

FIRST PRINTING—NOVEMBER 1976

Copyright © 1976 by TAB BOOKS

Printed in the United States
of America

Hardbound Edition: International Standard Book No. 0-8306-6769-5

Paperbound Edition: International Standard Book No. 0-8306-5769-X

Library of Congress Card Number: 76-45063

Library of Congress Cataloging in Publication Data

Harris, Morgan.
   How to make news & influence people.

   Bibliography: p.
   Includes index.
   1. Public relations. 2. Publicity. I. Karp,
Patti, joint author. II. Title.
HM263.H344   659.2   76-45063
ISBN 0-8306-6769-5
ISBN 0-8306-5769-X (pbk.)

Preface

There are lots of words used to describe the process by which everyday people make their news known: public relations, publicity, promotion, advertising. The words sometimes make the process sound complicated and difficult to execute. But there is no great mystery involved.

The object of the process is to get a certain message to reach a desired audience. To reach that goal, the club publicity chairman or public relations director really only needs to know some basic information, organize that information, and proceed according to logical steps. This book shows how to do it—easily.

Actually, the publicity chairman of an organization is a powerful individual. He or she has the opportunity to create an image for an entire group—and even, in some instances, a self-image for members of that group. The successful publicity chairman will get the organization's name and events into the public's awareness by using newspapers, TV, and radio media, as well as various advertising techniques like billboards, stickers, stunts, parades, posters, or brochures.

This book is intended to simplify the entire procedure. Starting from the basics of writing a news story, the book proceeds to unveil the process of planning a full-scale publicity program of campaign.

A "style manual" is included for those uncertain about newspaper conventions regarding format, punctuation, forms of address and the like. Elements of photography are detailed, along with tips on how to get a newspaper editor to supply a photographer. The book supplies information on how to get photographs and news stories published.

Radio and TV broadcasts are another good outlet for news, and the book covers how to go about using these media to your best advantage.

As with most other activities, getting publicity is governed to some extent by the finances available. For this reason, budgets—their creation, adoption, and use—are also detailed.

A guidebook of source material included in the back of this book is offered as a manual of practical instruction for the beginner and as a reference handbook for the experienced publicity chairman.

In short, the job of publicity chairman is a very important one. But, as this shows, the job can also be a simple one.

Morgan Harris
Patti Karp

Contents

Chapter 1

The Nature of Publicity

In Hollywood there is a legend that once upon a time the two kingpins of Metro-Goldwyn-Mayer had a disagreement which developed into a prolonged feud. During this time they did not speak to each other. Most of the top brass took sides, but one junior executive, recognizing an opportunity, did not join either faction. Instead he moved into a vacant office and had his name lettered on the door with the title "General Manager."

When a representative of Sam Goldwyn confronted him and demanded to know what he thought he was up to, he said, "You'll have to see Mr. Mayer about that." Then when one of Louis B. Mayer's men challenged him, he said, "You'll have to take that up with Mr. Goldwyn."

The feud finally came to an end, and when the two parties had settled their differences the first thing they did was make preparations to throw him out. They need not have bothered.

As "general manager" of M-G-M he had negotiated with other studios and had received some attractive offers, one of which he accepted. By the time his name and title were scraped off the office door at M-G-M he was functioning as a top executive in another studio.

If there ever was such a person, the studio that employed him got a man who knew how to create a public image with written words and how to transform it into reality. He would have made a fine publicist.

WHAT'S THE DIFFERENCE?

Question: What's the difference between publicity, advertising, and promotion?

Answer: Publicity appears in free space or on free time, consequently the producer of it does not have much control over it. Advertising, by contrast, is paid for and so the producer can specify where it is to appear and when.

Publicity tells a story and calls attention to the product or activity, but it does not usually contain a direct sales pitch. Advertising tells the story with the avowed purpose of selling goods, services, or ideas.

Promotion covers the field, including both publicity and advertising.

Question: What is the best way to put on a promotion campaign?

Answer: The best way is to employ an advertising agency to design and implement your entire advertising-promotional program.

Question: And if we can't afford an agency?

Answer: Then find professionals among your members or your friends who can help you and get services donated. Follow their advice. Find a commercial artist who can make designs and layouts.

Question: My church is having an "open house" this spring, and I am in charge of publicity and promotion. Where do I start?

Answer: Budgets come first. Find out how much you have to spend. Then obtain information to help you decide on newspaper advertising, magazines, radio, television, outdoor posters, direct mail, displays, and other channels. Plan your entire program in advance.

PUBLICITY IS EASY

Although there are many dramatic incidents in the field of publicity and promotion, most of it is much more simple and straightforward. With this book you will find out how it is done and how easy it is. With its help you'll find it's easier to succeed than to fail. By the time you have read this book once, you'll know more about publicity than most publicity chairmen. By the time you have used it as a reference and guidebook through the routes of publicity and applied the techniques it gives you, you will not only know *how* to do the job but how to do it the *easy way*.

Whether you were surprised when they appointed you, as some publicity chairmen have been, or whether you volunteered for the post, now that you are "it" you have opportunities that are not available to anyone else. As publicity chairman you hold a position with unequaled power.

You can create the kind of organization you want. You will determine, perhaps more than any other person besides the chairman, what direction the organization is going to take. Your viewpoint is needed in planning the events that make up the program. You will be there when plans are initiated, helping shape the activities so they will create the public image you and the other club officers want.

Then, with words and news stories, announcements and brochures, and TV shots and radio messages, you will sketch in the picture of the organization. And it will tend to fill in the sketches you have made.

In part this is because people can't help imitating. They tend to act out what others say of them and what they believe of themselves. And you can help them believe. Your publicity releases will be a mirror of the organization. The members will see themselves and their organization in that mirror, and they will tend to live up to what they see there—the image you have created.

PUBLICITY IS MAGIC

You may be pleasantly surprised to find that as publicity chairman you are something of a magician. Starting with a vision of what might be, you can apply the alchemy of the creative process by using the techniques in this handbook. Your ideas, expressed in words, will take shape and become the real world. Although creativity remains always a wonder and a mystery, even to its practitioners, you will watch your vision become reality as time goes by—a truly satisfying experience.

It's up-to-date. It's now. It deals with what is going on and what is coming up. It is an exciting job because you are creating the future.

It gives you wonderful opportunities to meet and work with creative people: artists and printers and writers, entertainers and reporters and lecturers, and radio and TV people. It will challenge and stimulate your own creativity.

Abraham Lincoln said, "With public sentiment, nothing can fail; without it, nothing can succeed. Consequently, he who molds public sentiment goes deeper than he who enacts statutes or pronounces decisions."

Although publicity makes things succeed, its value is not always appreciated. The stories you place in the paper and the TV and radio announcements have a substantial value. Commercial advertisers pay well for space in the paper and for time on the air.

If you want to calculate the cash value of this part of your contribution, get a rate card for display advertising from a local newspaper and figure out the amount it would cost to buy the number of column inches of stories and pictures you place in the paper. Do the same thing for your radio and TV time.

Of course this is only part of the value of your services to the organization. It is not easy to place a cash value on the brochures, posters, newsletters, and other things that you produce. They have a value that is beyond calculation. Who can measure what it's worth to make dreams come true?

PUBLICITY REQUIRES AUTHORITY

Publicity and public relations cover all the impressions made by an organization on every person—both those outside the organization and those who are a part of it. Sometimes the most important work of a publicity chairman is creating the right impressions, attitudes, ideas, and enthusiasm among the members of the organization itself. This requires tact and an affirmative approach. Napoleon Hill, author of *Think and Grow Rich*, said, "Nothing on earth will cause me to work so long or so hard as will sincere appreciation." Try it.

It also requires that the position of publicity chairman carry prestige. This means that (while not being filled with pride about your own personal importance) you appreciate the importance of the position and conduct yourself with the dignity and graciousness appropriate to the role. It means that you appreciate its challenges, its opportunity, its power, and its responsibility so thoroughly that you can forget yourself in doing the job with an enthusiasm and confidence that will be contagious. This will generate enthusiasm in members too, and they will have confidence in you.

The work of the publicity chairman is subordinate only to the chairman or president—no one else. You have been appointed to that post to write the stories, plan the campaigns, and create the printed and the broadcast material. Do not accept the position until there is a clear understanding and agreement that only one other person is to evaluate and approve your stories—probably the president—and that no other person is to write them. Two people cannot type on a typewriter at the same time: writing a story is a one person job. You are that person.

GETTING WHAT YOU WANT

Public relations is a matter of getting what you want from other people by giving them what they want. It's as simple as that. What you want as publicity chairman is a good public image for your club or organization. You want stories in the newspaper, and the way to get them is to give the editor what he wants. He wants people to read his paper, so he tries to give the readers what they want. This is the rule he works on.

So if you will give him the kind of stories his readers want, he will publish them. This book tells you what readers (and editors) want, and how to present it so they will like it.

PUBLICITY IS AN ART

Publicity is one of the great creative arts which turns ideas into words and turns words into reality. As publicity chairman you will be learning and practicing its techniques.

At the end of your first year you will be a more creative person, more knowledgeable, and more competent. You'll have more contacts, more friends, and more influence in both your organization and your community.

YOU CAN DO IT!

Let's hope that it won't be your last year. You will know the ropes. You will be an expert. If you want to, you can go on to be a professional.

But possibly there is more to the job of publicity chairman than you thought: more to be learned, more work perhaps, more fun, more challenge, more power, and more living. However, you will find it's a rewarding job. And best of all, you will prove that you can do it. More power to you.

Chapter 2

How To Plan
a Publicity Program

In building anything worthwhile you start with a blueprint. But before you can draw up the blueprint you must define the goal. This is the first step to success in any undertaking.

DEFINE THE GOAL

What are you trying to do as publicity chairman? The answer depends on what the purpose of your organization is. To get this more clearly in mind—not only your mind, but also in the minds of the officers and members—get on the agenda of the first meeting of the year and ask some questions: What are the permanent goals of our organization this year? List possible goals: members, money, successful support of certain projects, a cleaner environment, more fun for members, education for a peaceful world order, better race relations, election of more (Democrats or Republicans) to office, a successful nursery school, or whatever the officers and members want to set as goals.

How can publicity help us achieve these goals? What new publicity plans (in addition to the regular program) will contribute toward achieving our goals? Do members need a basic brochure containing a statement of the history of the organization, what it is at present, what its purposes are, and so forth? What other needs and what other suggestions do members have that should be included in the publicity program? Make notes on the answers and suggestions and take them home with you to use in defining your goals.

Your organization may already have a basic brochure which sets forth its goals in a clear and comprehensive statement. Maybe you can use this, but before you decide to do so, work out your own statement. You may come up with something better; at least you will come up with a fresh statement, and this is important. No matter how good a thing is, it must be periodically renewed; the breath of life must be breathed into it again and again.

In any case, start with a statement of the goals of the club and another statement of your goals as publicity chairman. Post these where you will see them whenever you sit down to work on publicity.

NAIL IT DOWN WITH A PLAN

Having defined your goals, your second step is to work out a comprehensive plan. Before you prepare a single piece of copy, lay out a brochure, schedule a photographer, or consider the use of computerized skywriting. You should plan the entire club year.

If you were working on a worldwide campaign complete with press conferences via TV satellite, you would not question the need of a plan. But if yours is a small club in a small town—or a small organization in a big city—you may be tempted to think the job is so small it doesn't need a plan: just turn in a news story to the paper once a month, and that's it.

Well, that's not it! You can spend a whole month trying to get a little story ready for the newspaper—if your work is not organized. And the essential step in organizing work is a plan. If the publicity chairman who preceded you got that story out in a couple of days at most and had no *written* plan, don't think he didn't have a plan. It may have been in his mind. But if he was efficient, he must have worked according to a plan. And so must you. Don't try to keep your plan in your head, even if he did. Write it down. This puts you in control. You won't get caught with a big event coming up and suddenly realize that the newspaper deadline for the advance story is 4 o'clock this afternoon and you have invited friends for dinner this evening and it's already noon!

To make planning easy divide it into three steps: (1) organize, (2) schedule, and (3) arrange. Organize your materials and equipment. Schedule your dates and times. Arrange with people to do their thing—their part of the program.

ORGANIZE YOUR MATERIALS AND EQUIPMENT

With the right equipment you'll get more work done, you'll get it done more easily, you'll save time, and you'll avoid frustration. There is great satisfaction in being able to do a job right, but this requires the right tools and materials.

So when it comes to buying equipment, don't stint. Get what you need. It is poor economy to try to save money at the cost of wasting your most valuable asset—your time. The reason modern devices, materials, and equipment have been invented and produced is to save time. Use them.

But don't pay for them yourself. You are giving your time—that's enough. Let the club treasury pay for the equipment you need. You can arrange to have a petty cash advance which you can spend for what you need. This fund is replenished by the treasurer when you turn in receipts showing what you have spent. Or you can have an arrangement whereby you lay out the money yourself for what you need, and you are reimbursed when you turn in the receipts.

But first be sure you do have an arrangement, a clear understanding between the president, the treasurer, and yourself about your budget—how much you are authorized to spend and how you are to be reimbursed. Incidentally, if your publicity work for the club is going to increase your phone bill, include that cost in the financial arrangement.

THINGS YOU'LL NEED

After (not before) the question of your budget is settled, you can go shopping. Here's what you'll need:

1. A giant calendar, about 18 × 20 inches with lots of white space around the numerals for each day so you can note programs, times, and places for the entire year. This enables you to see, for a month at a time, what things are coming up that require your attention.
2. A datebook, about 6 × 9 inches. Some of these have a week on a page, and some have a week spread over the double page. Some publicity chairmen prefer to have their datebook a part of a looseleaf notebook.

3. A looseleaf notebook, about 7 × 10 inches or perhaps 6 × 9 inches, with divisions for a phone list, newspaper list (addresses, phones, people, deadlines, etc.), radio and TV lists, several tabbed guide sheets which you can fill out to suit your own needs, and calendar sheets, if you choose this instead of having a separate datebook. Carry this notebook and your datebook with you at all times for quick reference and for immediate jotting down of items and ideas as they come to mind.

4. A scrapbook of "success stories" in which you keep all your news, advertisements, posters, invitations, newsphotos, releases, and other material you produce as publicity chairman. Make a copy of each story, whether it appears in the paper or not. Put the copy with the clippings of those stories that are published. Instead of a "success stories" book, you may want to call this your "good news" book.

If you don't like to mess with paste, you don't have to. You can buy "protector sheets"—clear plastic double pages into which you can slip the items you want to save. You can make these protector sheets do double duty by putting two items in *each*, one facing either way. They come with holes so they can be kept in a standard three-ring binder.

If you are fortunate enough to inherit a scrapbook from your predecessor containing stories and other items produced, you'll find it a big help. But don't rely on it so much that it interferes with your own creativity. In any case, see that your successor inherits yours; it will make his job that much easier.

5. A scrapbook in which to keep good model stories that you find in the paper. Of course you can keep these in the "success stories" scrapbook by putting in a cardboard divider with a tab to separate the book into two parts.

6. Two dozen manila folders in an accordian holder or in a metal box built to hold file folders. This is to file correspondence, extra copies of news stories, etc.

7. A file box and 3 × 5-inch cards together with a set of alphabetical tab cards. You may want to make out some additional guide cards with the tabs labeled *Typing, Phoning, Photographs,* and the like. Behind

each of these guides in your file box will be cards giving the names, addresses, and phone numbers of members who can help you at the tasks of phoning, typing, and getting pictures. See the section on "Talent Card File" further on in this chapter for more details.

If there is not already a pocket inside the cover of your looseleaf notebook, you can buy a three-hole plastic pocket to fit. In it, carry a supply of 3 × 5-inch cards. If you have an idea, need an address, or have to pass a note to someone during a meeting, these cards are ideal.

Get the habit of writing things down. The dullest pencil is sharper than the sharpest memory.

8. Typing paper, carbon paper, letterheads, envelopes, and stamps. One step toward starting the year right is to put a new ribbon in your typewriter. And replace it often enough so your typing looks good. Sharp-looking typing may not seem to create a strongly favorable impression, but gray typing from a worn ribbon certainly creates a negative impression. Also, buy a supply of new carbon paper. Fuzzy, dirty carbons are an abomination.

If you have the habit of erasing your typing mistakes, swear off. You can get little tabs of paper with chalk on one side from the stationery store. These can be inserted quickly over the typing; when you strike over the error the white chalk covers it up beautifully. Also get a small bottle of white correction fluid that can be painted over typing.

SCHEDULE DATES AND TIMES

Your master publicity plan will work better if you have a visual program to follow. Your giant calendar will enable you to see ahead what is coming up and what you have to do to prepare for it.

Fill out the calendar for the entire club year, listing the regular meeting dates. Write a memo about each one a few days before the meeting date as a reminder. If you plan to send out a news story about any of these meetings, note on your calendar the day the story is to be written and the newspaper deadline for it. Also list on the calendar the dates of special events that are planned. If the date is tentative, write it in pencil. When it is confirmed, write it in ink. Write in a schedule of the news releases you wish published. Schedule dates and times around the paper's deadlines.

Your club president probably maintains a master calendar with which your own calendar should be correlated.

Count Back

When you enter a special event, "count back" to the date you want publicity to start. If you are planning a play, count back a couple of months before the opening to locate the date you want your publicity story to appear which will give the name of the play and the date of the first performance. Note this on the calendar. Then count back from that to the preceding deadline of the newspaper. Note that, and count back to the day you want to write the story and get it to the paper. Follow this procedure in making a timetable for all the special events.

If the nominating committee is going to report on a certain date, count back to the day you want to ask the chairman for biographical information about the candidates, so you can include it in the story of the announcement.

Do not surprise people by announcing winners at meetings. Announce them in a news story before the meeting; you will have greater attendance at the meeting.

Your Datebook

The datebook and the calendar come close to duplicating each other. The datebook you will carry with you, and you can make entries in it during club meetings or wherever you are when ideas occur to you. These can then be copied onto the calendar which is your visible reminder—always in front of you, on your desk or on the wall.

Use your datebook at the first meeting to write down a tentative schedule for the entire year. List all regular events and special activities, and make notations on the days that you have to do things prior to these events and activities.

Once you have written the items in your datebook, you don't have to worry about remembering them. Your mind is then free to consider the business at hand.

The datebook serves a double function. First, it is a place to record things as they come up, so they will not be forgotten. Second, it is a source book to refer to whenever needed. With it you will always be ready to meet with club officers at a moment's notice, prepared to suggest the next step in the year's publicity program.

Put your name and address on the front of it.

Balance The Year's Program

To keep the public image of your organization alive in people's minds—and with your members, as well—you need to maintain a continuous flow of news stories. When you have completed listing the various events on your calendar, look at it to see if there are dead periods during which no newsworthy events are happening for several weeks. Fill in these "holes" in the year's program.

Go over the schedule with the program chairman to see whether two events are scheduled so close together that one of them could be moved to a blank spot in the year. Or perhaps a special activity can be planned to take advantage of the lull.

To fill a blank spot you can have the club president, or the club itself, issue a statement on some current public issue. This is more likely to be newsworthy if it is a local issue in your town or county rather than some nationwide or worldwide issue. The statement should be related to some recent news event or happening in your community.

During blank publicity periods you can issue stories on forthcoming events, or on current events that are related to forthcoming events. For instance, you can write a story about an executive committee meeting to plan for a fund-raising program later in the year.

If you can't spead events to cover blank periods, you can spread the publicity.

Suppose your club is presenting a play in May, and you have planned your first news release about it to go out two months in advance—in March. But your calendar shows a big hole with nothing newsworthy in January or February. You can put out an announcement in January about the selection of the play. In February you can have a followup story announcing tryouts for the cast.

By one means or another keep the stories going out. And don't be discouraged it they are not all published. You are keeping your organization alive in the mind of the editor and perhaps building up pressure for him to publish your stories. If he has rejected two of your stories (and published stories from other organizations) he may feel it is necessary to print the next one you send in just to be fair.

Bulletin Board

"Internal publicity" is the basis of good external public relations. Don't neglect it. Your members are most important part of your audience; you are writing for the effect on them as well as for the effect on outsiders.

Therefore, if there is not already a bulletin board, get one put up and post on it copies of your news stories, clippings of the stories that are published, pictures, announcements, programs, and notes of appreciation (usually your appreciation of what a member has done). Sometimes you may post a letter to the club expressing the gratitude of the writer for some club activity. Keep on this board anything that will help members appreciate and take pride in their club.
Also post the things that will help them know what is happening and what is going to happen. Get an intriguing name for this board, such as "What And Who Board."

Work Way Ahead

Timing is one of the secrets of success. To stay on top of your job—instead of letting it get on top of you—plan and work far in advance of deadlines. Make your appointments, carry out your interviews, order your printing, and begin writing your stories much earlier than necessary.

If certain information is not available until the last moment, that doesn't mean that you have to wait until the last moment to write your story. You can get the story written and leave a blank space in which to fill in, for example, the title of the lecture when the speaker sends it to you. Working well ahead of schedule will give you breathing space, it will give you power, and it will keep you in control.

ARRANGE WITH PEOPLE

The cynic was wrong who said, "It's not so much *what* you know as *who* you know." The truth is that you must know *both* *what* and *who*: *what* to do and *whom* to turn to for information or help in doing it. Your contacts are just as important to your success as your own knowledge and skill. So make a card file listing everyone you will work with while you are publicity chairman.

It may be useful to classify your contacts as to whether they are sources or outlets. The sources are all the people from whom you get information, materials, and services. The outlets are those to whom you send news stories, announcements, posters, and letters—those through whom your message will be relayed to the people you are trying to reach. You may be trying to reach the general public or a certain segment of the public: the prospects to whom you are trying to sell tickets, ideas, purposes, membership in your club, or whatever.

List of Source People

Get a complete, up-to-date membership list from the club secretary. In addition to the full names of the members, this list should show the full first names and initials of spouses. This may not be important to anyone else, but it is a must for the publicity chairman to have these names.

At the first meeting of the year, ask everyone to correct any errors in the way their names are listed and to bring the listing of their phone numbers and addresses up to date, including zip codes. Have the secretary get this information from those who are absent so that your list will be complete and accurate.

Other individuals on your list of sources from whom you get information and help are regional and national officers of your organization, printers, photographers, sign painters and poster designers, typists, friends who'll help, and others. Local celebrities and VIPs who will pose for publicity pictures with members of your group should also be included.

Talent Card File

Make up a card file of club members who can do special jobs. Get some 3 × 5-inch cards with blank tabs and list on them the type of job, such as *Typing*. Behind that card, file cards containing the names, addresses, and phone numbers of individuals who can do typing for you. On each card put a note telling when the person can work and other data you will need to have before you phone them.

Another tab should list *Telephoning* and another *Photography*. What classifications you will have will depend on the kind of job you want done and on the available manpower. Some tabs may include several kinds of jobs which are related, such as *Layout*. Behind this tab you may file cards of people who can do pasteup, hand lettering, posters, plans or blueprints, commercial art, and drawings on stencils.

You may have a tab labeled *Shows*, and the cards behind it will include people who can serve as stage crew, do stage design, paint scenery, and sew costumes. It may list poets who can write songs for your events or verse for special occasions, someone who can operate a puppet theater, or carpenters who can build stage sets or temporary room dividers.

You may have a tab labeled *Printing* behind which you will file cards for individuals who can write specifications for printing, make layouts, do pasteups, etc. You may want to make several cards and file them under several different headings for some people. For instance, a person who can do pasteups might be filed under *Printing* and also under *Layouts*.

List people who can distribute handbills, monitor radio and TV stations, write news stories or advertising copy or letters, put up posters, do filing, etc.

List of Outlet People

First on this list are newspaper editors, program directors of radio and TV stations, and other key people in media. Make this *master press list* one of your first jobs.

Your list of outlets should include anyone to whom you send news stories and announcements: chairmen of other clubs, ministers, editors of church bulletins, librarians, school principals, and others whom you may want to ask to post notices on bulletin boards. List the names of each of these people on a 3 × 5-inch card with full information. An example follows:

ROBERTS, John Arnold   phone: 289-5936
Editor, Hearthside Press
1012 Twentieth Street
Formerstone, California 90292
Secretary's name: Jaqueline Donalds

You may also want notations on these cards to help you in getting along with these people and keeping them happy. For instance, if your organization is one that normally sends Christmas cards or gifts you may want to note, for example, that this one is allergic to chocolate and that one does not drink. Or if a person works late and rises late, you may have a notation "Do not phone before 11 a.m." On some cards you may want to list both a business address and phone and a home address and phone.

For John Arnold Roberts, listed previously, you may want two other cards: one for HEARTHSIDE PRESS, and another one for DONALDS, Jacqueline. You can avoid duplication (in mailings to this list, for instance) by making out an original on a white card and making out the other listings on colored cards. You can get blue, orange, pink, and other colored 3 × 5-inch cards from the stationery store.

Send Them Tickets

Whenever you are having an event to which you can invite any of these people, send them tickets, invitations, or announcements.

These aren't the "big shots" and the VIPs. They are the secretaries, the assistants and aides, the caretakers, and maintenance personnel. It may be to your advantage to make friends of these people.

The janitor or the caretaker may know where things are and how to get at them and frequently knows a great deal then most people suspect. Treat him with respect and you may be surprised at the response you will get and the help he can give you.

Increase Your Face Value: Smile

Making a card file of your contacts and keeping it up-to-date is essential. But more important than this—more important than any of these techniques of organization—is to keep constantly in mind that each of your contacts is a human being who needs encouragement, appreciation, and friendship, someone who is looking for and will respond quickly to a friendly word and a smile.

Everyone in our society is looking for what psychologists call "identity." Everyone wants to be somebody, wants to be recognized for the really fine, beautiful person that he or she is. And if you are the one who recognizes an individual's true worth, who expresses a sincere interest in him, he will respond to you with friendship and cooperation.

And when your job as publicity chairman comes to an end you will retain—as a kind of reward—the friends you have made.

Keep a Record of Successes

After you have worked out your goals and your plan for accomplishing those goals, organized your materials, scheduled the dates and times of events, and planned your stories you are ready to shoot for the target and to make your first bull's-eye.

As news releases, announcements, posters, and letters go out, put copies or pictures of them in your scrapbook of success stories. Clip the stories that are published and put them with the copies.

Your plan is like an advance story for your total program. Your scrapbook is the cover story, showing how much of the plan was executed and how much of it reached its audience through the newspapers, radio, TV, bulletin boards, or other media.

A small community-based newspaper rarely publishes even half the stories submitted to it. A large metropolitan paper publishes even a smaller proportion. Most stories received by the editor finish up in his wastebasket just because he does not have room in the paper for them. So when you send in five stories, if one or two of them are published, smile. You are doing great! That's success for a publicity chairman.

Chapter 3
How To Write
a News Story

The stories that interest everybody go on the front page. Those that interest a good many people go on the inside pages, at the top of the column. Those that interest only a few go further back in the paper, lower down in the column, and get less space. The stories most people won't want to bother to read go in the wastebasket.

MORE STORIES THAN SPACE

Because your newspaper editor gets far more stories than he has space for, he has to decide which stories go on the front page, which stories go on the inside pages, and which stories go into the wastebasket.

Whether people will want to read your story depends on (1) the facts in the story, (2) the way those facts are presented, and (3) timeliness. This defines your task: (1) get the facts and get them right (the first time), (2) present them in a readable story, and (3) get the story to the paper on time. And what makes a story readable? News.

WHAT'S NEWS?

News is what people want to read, what they are curious about, what happened, and what is going to happen. News is a report of where the action is. In your organization it's regular events that are coming up, it's things that have just happened, it's special events, it's unusual items, and it's people—always people.

NAMES MAKE NEWS

People want to see their names in the paper. They also want to see their friends' names in the paper. They want to know "who." (The handling of names in news stories is a little tricky, so check Chapter 4, "Names Make News.")

A news story is usually about people, what they have done or what they are going to do. It answers questions about six items which have been put into verse by Rudyard Kipling to help you remember them easily:

> I keep six honest serving men (They taught me all I knew.)
> Their names are What and Why and When
> And How and Where and Who.

Here is an illustration of how you might use these in a story:

> What —The annual pancake breakfast sponsored
> Who— by the Newton Council for Survival Research
> What — will be served starting 7 o'clock Saturday morning, August 14, in the
> Where—dining hall of the Masonic Club on Elm Street.
> Why —The proceeds will be used to purchase furnishings for the Boy Scout camp at Mohawk Lake.
>
> Another
> Who — Mr. Arthur Stall, president of the council.
>
> Another
> Who— announced that Emory Campbell and Dare Smith will be chefs, and they promise "all the pancakes and bacon you can eat."

In this story the question "How?" is not answered because there is no question about this in the reader's mind. Sometimes an item may be omitted because the information is not known. But while you are writing your news story, check it against this list to see if you have covered each of the items the reader will want to know about.

These are the ingredients of a story; now how do you put them together?

WHAT COMES FIRST?

Everything comes first. You tell the whole story in the first sentence—or at least in the first paragraph . This is called the *lead*.

The second paragraph goes over the story again, filling in details. The third paragraph contains more details, which are not so important. As you go on through the story, it gives more and more information that is less and less important.

This is called an *inverted pyramid*: the big stuff is at the top and the story peters out to nothing at the end. The reason for this is that newspapers are made up in a hurry, so as to get them into the hands of the readers while the news is current. The printed story comes to the editor on long proof sheets called galleys. The printed story he is trying to fit onto the page may be longer than the space he has for it. There is not time to send it back to be rewritten shorter and set in type again. So what does he do? He throws away the last paragraph or last few lines. And if an advertisement comes in at the last moment, that goes on the page and he throws away some more copy from the bottom of your story.

Your story must be written so that the final paragraphs can be thrown away. That is why the lead paragraph should be a complete story. So pack the whole thing into the first paragraph. Then expand on it.

Some editors get so many stories they have only time to read the first paragraph. From that they judge the rest of the story. If the lead paragraph is weak, the editor may conclude that the entire story should go into the wastebasket.

WHY NOT INTO THE NEWSPAPER?

Most press releases are thrown away because (1) the subject is not of enough interest to enough readers, (2) they are poorly written, or (3) they are not timely. As you plan your news releases you should be asking, "Why will the general reader be interested in this?" And as you write your news release you should be asking "How can I say this so the general reader will find it readable?"

Note that you do *not* ask "How can I say this so the general reader will find it *interesting*?" The interest is in the subject, in the facts you present, not in the way you present them. If the reader is not interested in the Council for Survival Research or the Boy Scouts or in Arthur Stall, Emory Campbell, or Dare Smith, and if he is not interested in breakfast on Saturday morning, there is no use trying by some tricky writing to interest him in that news story.

The question is "How can I say this so the reader (who has some slight interest in some of these facts) will find it readable?" The answer is "Say it simply!" What is called for in news stories is brevity, precision, an an accurate presentation of the facts in the order of their importance. That's it.

And that's all. If the reader is not interested in the facts you have to report, there is almost nothing you can do to make him interested. Don't try. Just give the facts. Your story will then have the best chance of being published and read. And the editor will come to appreciate you as a trustworthy, competant source of news for his paper.

HOW LONG SHOULD YOUR COPY BE?

Your story shouldn't be long; it should be short. How short? Get it on two pages if possible.

Type it in a narrow column, about 35 characters per line to correspond with the average newspaper column line. This will give the editor some idea how many printed lines the story will make. Actually a story should be just long enough to tell what it has to say—and no longer. Don't pad it. Don't put in unnecessary words. Tell who, what, when, how, and why plainly and briefly. Give facts: dates, names, titles, addresses, times, scores, numbers, and deadlines.

Be specific. Don't write generalities such as "The picnic was attended by a large number of people." How many is "a large number" for goodness sake? Say, "120 people." If you didn't count them, make an estimate. It's better to make up a figure than to write a generality. Or you can write "more than 100 people." Or you can say "a crowd estimated to be 120 people."

The final paragraphs can be more general, perhaps giving the history of your organization or some recent statistics. This will leave the editor something to cut if he has to.

LETTERS TO THE EDITOR

News stories are facts, not opinions. When opinion is written it is classified as "editoral" matter. The editor's and publisher's opinions are printed in editorial columns. If your paper has a column called "letters to the editor," that's where reader opinion will be printed.

This column can sometimes be used to get publicity. A letter of appreciation or commendation—such as a thank you letter for press coverage of a special event—is likely to be published. The editor gets so much criticism, he likes to be able to show that some people appreciate his paper. In such a letter you can get in a sentence or a paragraph that mentions the purpose of your organization.

Letters in this column frequently express the opinion of the writer on some subject that is currently in the news. If your organization is doing something about this subject, it can get favorable mention in such a letter. Sometimes it may be best if the letter does not appear over your signature; have some other person write it. You are a source of news for the paper, and you want the editor to gain confidence in what you write. He must know that you give FACTS, not opinion.

Actually, it is almost impossible to get anyone to write a letter. So what you do is to write the letter for him, get him to sign it, and send it in. But don't overwork this gimmick.

Sometimes an opinion is news—if it is the opinion of a VIP. If the mayor thinks the streets of the town need repairing, that's his opinion, but it is also news because people want to know what the mayor thinks. If you mention someone in your news story whose opinion will be of interest to the readers of the paper, put it in as a quotation.

DON'T REWRITE THE WHOLE STORY

Try to avoid sending exactly the same story to several newspapers. If an editor finds in another paper the same story he has printed in his, he won't like it. Nor would you if you were an editor and the members of your service club started accusing you of copying your stories from your competitor.

If you do send the same release to more than one publisher, type "Distribution" at the top and list all the outlets you are sending it to. This will warn the editor that he had better rewrite your copy if he wants an original story.

Better still, if there are several newspapers in your area, write a different story for each of them. But you don't have to rewrite the entire story. If you will write a different lead—a different opening paragraph for each of them—the balance of the story can be the same or practically the same.

The same with pictures. Send *different* photos of the same event to different newspapers—with different captions, of course.

THREE DIFFERENT LEADS

Here are three different leads for the same story—for three different newspapers published in the same area:

—1—

The Thomas Jefferson Research Center is offering a workshop in Emotional Maturity Instruction on 16 Tuesday evenings beginning January 27 at the Center's headquarters on North Lake Avenue in Pasadena. The workshops are open to the public at a fee of $25.

Frank Goble. president of the center. says. "This is the program that has achieved national acclaim for its results in the rehabilitation of inmates at the Georgia prison system. and equally dramatic results in schools and churches throughout the country with people who are troubled with marriage problems. drug problems. and psychological problems of all kinds.

"This is the fourth workshop we have presented. and there has been an enthusiastic response from all who have attended. with increased attendance at each one." (more)

—2—

The fourth workshop in Emotional Maturity Instruction will start Tuesday evening. January 28. at the headquarters of the Thomas Jefferson Research Center. North Lake Avenue. Pasadena. Sixteen sessions are offered at a fee of $25. All are welcome. (more)

—3—

Opening Tuesday evening. January 27. a 16-week workshop on Emotional Maturity Instruction will be offered to the public at the headquarters of the Thomas Jefferson Research Center. North Lake Avenue. Pasedena. The fee for the entire workshop is $25. but visitors are invited to attend the first evening before making up their mind to enroll.

DON'T BOTHER WITH HEADLINES

Fortunately. you don't have to write the headline. A headline writer at the newspaper will do that. You're lucky. because writing headlines is a difficult job on a newspaper. Just leave space—plenty of space—on the paper above your story where the headline can be written.

You can write about all the recurring events your organization has: election of officers. installation of officers.

annual picnics, contests, and annual campaigns—everything except regular meetings should have at least two stories. You can write one before the event, telling what is going to happen; and you can write the other after the event—*immediately* after—telling what happened, unless the newspaper has sent its own reporter to the event.

Regular meetings do not take a story. Instead, send the newspaper a "meeting notice" form as shown in Chapter 5.

What else do you write about? You write about special events such as sponsoring a charity ball, presenting a speaker, having a parade, or offering a course in parent-child relations. You might write about a sale, a theater party, a fashion show, a sports car rally, a pancake breakfast, a charter flight, a cleanup campaign, a pet show, a tournament, or a festival—any special event.

To get the greatest number of people to attend, you will want to write several stories about it. The first one is likely to be the direct announcement of the event. But news must be new. So you can't just repeat the same announcement next week in different words. To get another story published about the same event, you need something different, a new angle.

These stories may tell about chairmen of committees who have been appointed, others who will be taking part, celebrities and guests who will be present, other organizations that may be participating, announcements of door prizes, food and menus, changes in plans, arrangements, or personnel. Watch for stories of a similar nature in your local newspaper, and keep a scrapbook filled with them. Look at them frequently for ideas.

Not all these stories will get in the paper. It's like planting seeds. Maybe every third seed will grow. You'll still get a good harvest.

CABLE FROM GOLDA INSPIRES VALLEY HADASSAH CAMPAIGN

A cable from Golda Meir, former Prime Minister of Israel, has sparked the second half of a month-long membership drive sponsored by The Eastern Interior Region of Hadassah.

Mrs. Abe Cohen, publicity chairman for the event, wrote to Mrs. Meir telling of the campaign and enclosed a copy of the invitation to the culminating Gala Art Festival. The former Prime Minister took time from her already overcrowded schedule to respond by sending a cable of best wishes and a few words of encouragement.

The Art Festival, a black tie evening under the direction of Mrs. Joseph Stein, will feature 25 prominent Los Angeles area artists displaying their work in the rotunda of Sam Luce at 1856 Drake Street, City.

Coordinating the efforts of the five chapters and all activities relative to the drive is Mrs. Avigdor Pearlman, who works under Mrs. Oscar Brant.

In the above example the publicity chairman's idea developed a followup story for a membership drive. The name Golda Meir practically guaranteed this story would be published: names make news. Observe that four other individuals are named in this brief 150-word story.

A story published in advance of an event telling what is going to happen at some future date is called an "advance story"—sometimes referred to as a "prewrite." When the event happens some reporter (probably you) covers it and writes the story telling what went on. This is called the "cover story"—sometimes referred to as a "postwrite."

AN INTERVIEW MAKES A GOOD FOLLOWUP

There are always more than enough stories to fill the newspaper. The editor has to choose. If you have sent him an interview with a picture of a VIP who is going to participate in a coming event scheduled by your club, and he has to choose between that and a run-of-the-mill story sent in by the publicity chairman of some other club, yours will be the story he publishes. Why? Because people like to eavesdrop. If questions are being asked of some noted person, they want to read the answers.

So if the speaker at your big event is near enough so that you can get to him, make an appointment to interview him. Go with your questions prepared. If you can take a cassette along and record the interview, fine. If that is not possible, take notes and write the interview immediately afterward. Don't take time to go home. Sit in the waiting room outside his office or in your car or anywhere you can go over your notes and write down everything you can remember. A half hour later you will have forgotten some things. Don't wait. Do it right away.

Later, when you go home, write the story you are going to submit, and follow similar stories in your scrapbook as models.

People who are unaccustomed to speaking before a microphone are frequently surprised how much it inhibits their free flow of talk. When you interview a person, you want him to be at ease. Therefore, find out whether he speaks at ease with a microphone. If not, don't use a tape recorder.

Some people freezeup when you even bring out a pen and note pad. If you are not sure of your person, it is best to get him talking first—ask some personal question, most people can talk about themselves easily. Then, when he is engrossed in a conversation you can quietly slip out your note pad and pen and begin making notes.

If the person you would like to interview is too far away for you to see him in person, you might be able to interview him over the phone. (Get your club to foot the phone bill.) Or you can write and ask if he would be willing to give you written (or taped) answers to eight or ten questions for use in an interview article. Most people are eager for publicity and will give you extensive and cordial cooperation.

THE PERSONALITY FEATURE

Newspaper readers would like to read about the leading lady in your club play or the designer who is arranging your fashion show. Give them a story about her life and activities, particularly those which relate to the program in which she is taking part. Accompany it with a picture, of course. Pattern your story after the stories in your scrapbook which you have clipped from the same paper in which you want your story to appear.

If the person has someone handling her publicity, or if she is with an organization which has a public relations office, you can get their help—information, photos, and even assistance in writing the story if you need it. If the publicist is being paid to keep his client's name and face in the public view, he will roll out the red carpet for anyone trying to get a photograph published or a news story about her in the paper.

THE HUMAN INTEREST STORY

Editors love to publish a human interest story because everybody is interested in reading it. It is a story about a person, but the personality is not the focus of the story. The human interest story zooms in on some event in the life of the person, one thing that happened to him in a situation that the reader is naturally interested in.

The human interest story has a universal appeal, that is, it doesn't matter whether it happened in your neighborhood or

1000 miles away; it will interest readers in big cities as well as those in small towns. It may be a story of children selling lemonade at the circus grounds and being bought off by the management with tickets to the circus. Or it may be a story of a dog that saves its owner's life or of a low-paid working person who inherits $100,000 from a laborer he once helped.

You can't just make up a human interest story to fit your needs, but if you can dig one out of the anecdotes told to you by the instructor who is going to teach the course in parent-child relationships offered by your club, it may get a choice spot in the paper and also swell the crowd that turns out to take the course.

GET THE FACTS

Whatever kind of story you are writing, get the facts: names, times, dates, and places. Get them right the first time, especially the names. All too often when the publicity chairman goes home after the meeting and sits down at his typewriter to write the story, he realizes he does not know how to spell the name of the honored guest. So he calls up the club president—who isn't home—and wastes a lot of time that he should have saved by getting the spelling of the name at the meeting.

KEEP A "NOW" NOTEBOOK

Take notes while the meeting is going on. Get the spelling of the names; that's the "who." Let your "six honest serving men" guide your note-taking so you also get the "what," the "when," the "where," the "how," and the "why." Always gather up copies of programs, menus, and announcements—any printed or duplicated material that is available.

Check on the facts *while you are there*. "Check" means confirm, ask, and be sure. It is fatal to think, "I'll find out about that later." A publicity chairman has to be a "now" person. Get it now.

Its also fatal to think, "I'll remember that." Put it down. Your notebook is your memory.

Doublecheck when you write the story to be sure you have it correct and complete. If you aren't positive about the middle initial or whether the address is a street or an avenue, look it up.

An event that is more than one day old is history. Schedule your time so that you can (1) write your story immediately after the event and (2) get it to the paper as soon as you have written it.

THE BEST IS GOOD ENOUGH

After you have been a publicity chairman for ten years. you can start being original. But don't try it yet. One of the marks of the amateur is the mistake of trying to do cute. clever. original writing. Don't do it. You'll get more stories published. your club president will be happier. and you'll be satisfied if you write plain, simple, clear, ordinary stories—the kind that you find in every issue of the newspaper.

Look at those stories. Cut out the ones that could serve you as good models and paste them in a scrapbook. Then when you find yourself stewing over how to write your story. look at the scrapbook and follow the form and style of one of the stories there. You probably can't improve on the best stories in the newspaper. but you can pattern your story after them and come up with one that is just as good as the best. And that's good enough.

Chapter 4

Names Make News

BEAUTIFUL WORDS

To almost everyone, the most beautiful sound in the world is his own name. Everyone loves to hear it spoken, to read it, and to know that to the writer or speaker we are at that moment the center of attention.

An individual will treasure an issue of a newspaper if it has his name in it. When a person's name appears in your newsletter, it makes that publication of greater interest and value to him.

Next in importance to his own name, a person is interested in reading the name of a friend or someone he knows. It gives the reader some identity and some status if he can say, "Oh, yes. I know that person."

Therefore, *names make news*. This is the reason community newspapers print lists of names of people who attend a gathering. If you don't know any of the people, you may think that list is such dull reading you wonder why they printed it. But those who do know some of the people or who were there will scan the list carefully looking for names they recognize.

GET IT RIGHT!

Because the person's name is so important to him, he is very much offended if you don't get it right. So get it right: get the spelling correct. If you are not sure what it is, ask the person himself or a member of his family.

If "Jr." appears after a man's name, remember that's part of the name. Never omit it.

You can use the full name—first, middle, and last—if that is how the person prefers to be identified. For example, Samuel Quincy Adams. Or you can use the first name and one initial: Samuel Q. Adams. Or you can use two initials: Mrs. E. V. Jones. But never use just one initial and the last name: Mrs. A. Garner. And never abbreviate a name: Sam Adams, Mrs. Jas. Holt, Pres. Chas. Arlington, Dr. Wm. Breckenridge.

FORMS OF ADDRESS

These forms of address are always abbreviated:

Singular	*Plural*
Mrs.	Mmes.
Mr.	Messrs.
Ms.	Mss.

These are written in full:

Miss	Misses

"Miss" generally should precede the names of unmarried women above high school age unless they prefer the modern form "Ms." For example, "Miss Evelyn Greer, honorary chairman." If there are two or more: "The Misses Alice Johnson and Ethel Williams, maids in waiting."

When naming a married woman or a widow, find out if she prefers to use her husband's first name: "Mrs. Jason Marmon." Or she may prefer her own first name: "Ethel Marmon."

A reference to two or more married women may read "Mmes. James Hobson and John Arbiter." There are exceptions to this rule; some feminists and professional women may insist on using their own first name: "Adela Rogers St. John" or "The Misses Mary Pickford and Loretta Young."

Because of difficulties and objections to forms of address that distinguish between married and unmarried women, a form that is growing in popularity is the term "Ms." The plural is "Mss."

The forms of address for men is simpler since there are no distinction between married and the unmarried; they are all addressed "Mr." The plural is "Messrs." "Messrs. Edborg Jackson and Arnold Dairlee, co-chairmen of the drive." In fact, many newspapers omit any form of address for a man—and some do for women too.

The following forms of address are abbreviated when they precede the full name: Gov., Sen., and Rep.

The title "Reverend" is an adjective, consequently it is preceded by "the," just as if one were saying, "the friendly Mr. Jackson." Never address a minister as "doctor" unless he has a doctor's degree. Abbreviate "Rev."

Use the term "Dr." for physicians, osteopaths, chiropractors, dentists, veterinarians, and individuals holding PhDs, EdDs, or other doctorates.

On a later reference to the same person in the story, spell out the form of address and omit the first name: "Speaking to the Conference of Mayors, Gov. Ronald Reagan of California said ... Following his address, Governor Reagan invited the mayors to visit the Capitol Building ...." or "Opening the ceremonies, the Rev. Luther Mott lead in prayer. At the close of the meeting, Rev. Mott pronounced the benediction."

Catholic priests and some Episcopal ministers are addressed as "Father." The full word is used the first time the person is mentioned, and the abbreviation "Fr." is used in subsequent references: "Father Joseph O'Connor agreed to return the following week ... Late in the afternoon Fr. O'Connor returned to the parish house."

Of course each newspaper has its own distinctive style. By regularly reading the newspapers you send copies to, you can take notes of the style preference of each.

TITLES FOLLOW THE NAME

Forms of address precede the name; titles often follow the name. The first time you mention a person in a news story, identify him completely with (1) proper form of address, (2) full name, and (3) title or other identifying reference: "Gen. Martin Braddock, president of the First National Bank ..." or "Mrs. Edward Draper, a history teacher at Harvey High School ...."

Later references to them in the story may use the forms of address and the last name: "General Braddock was appointed chairman for the first meeting" or "Mrs. Draper announced the prizewinners in the essay contest."

In listing people, mention first those individuals who are identified by a title, such as "master of ceremonies" or "floor manager," if they have not already been mentioned. The other names follow in alphabetical order: "Among those present were Mrs. Edmond Dirksen, chairman of the flower show, Donald Zander, treasurer, Miss Ethel Dancer, Mrs. Lucille Little, Mrs. Paul Morrison, and Mrs. John Zander."

If the title does precede the name, it is usually capitalized: "Chairman Joan Smith" or "President James Holt."

ABBREVIATIONS

As mentioned before, do not abbreviate the names of people. Names of states are abbreviated when they immediately follow the name of a city or town.

In abbreviating the names of well-known organizations, you may use periods or omit them: P.T.A. or PTA for Parent Teachers Association and B.S.A. or BSA for Boy Scouts of America. Be consistent within every story.

In giving addresses you may abbreviate the designation of thoroughfares, such as St. for street, Rt. for route, Ave. for avenue, Blvd. for boulevard, or Bldg. for building.

You may also abbreviate geographical names, such as Mt. Vernon, Ft. Dodge, and Ellsworth Pk.

Do not abbreviate the days of the week or names of the months in a news story: "A membership luncheon will be held in January."

WHEN TO USE CAPITAL LETTERS

Capital letters are signposts to help the writer make his meaning clear. All the rules for capitals are based on one simple idea: use a capital letter for the special name of one particular person, group of people, place, or thing.

Capitals for Personal Titles and Names

A word that shows a person's profession, rank, or office is called a title and it is capitalized when it precedes his name: "The presentation was made by President Jeremy A. Farnsworth, founder of Jason College." Do not capitalize a title that follows a person's name: "Prime Minister Golda Meir. honorary chairman of the event."

Capitals for Titles of Books and Plays

Capitalize the first word and all important words in titles of books. plays. speeches. movies. works of art. and musical compositions. "Gone with the Wind" and "An American Tragedy." Unless it is the first word in the title. do not capitalize a. an. and. but. for. in. of. or. the. to. or with.

Capitals for Nouns in Names

Capitalize nouns that apply to a particular one of their kind: parks. centers. camps. oceans. rivers. lakes. and mountains: "Blue Lake." "Evergreen Camp." "Humbolt Redwood Forest." and "Central Park."

Capitals for Organizations

Conform to the style used by the group. Capitalize the name of a particular club or organization. but do not capitalize the words *the, and, of, in, for,* and *to* unless it is the first word in the name. for example. the National Conference of Christians and Jews. Cub Scouts. Boy Scouts of America. The Red Cross. United Crusade. and Catholic Big Brothers.

Capitalize nouns and adjectives that apply to particular nationalities. languages. races. and religious groups: Interracial Center for Moslems. Christains. and Jews. The American Red Cross. The Red Man. Society of French Speakers. Negro Baptist Church. Southwest Indian Foundation. and Club Albania.

Capitals for Individual Institutions

Capitalize the names of particular companies. stores. buildings. hotels. theaters. schools: The First Methodist Church. Bonnie Bell Lodge. The Wilson Memorial Library. and Glendale Hospital.

Capitals for Particular Brands

Capitalize the names of particular brands of products. but do not capitalize the products: "The first prize was a Cookrite electric stove." Often newspapers will not use brand names.

Capitals for Calendar Items

Publicity writing is about people—one particular person or group of people doing things at a certain place at a particular time. Therefore, capitalize the days of the week, months, and holidays: "North Hollywood Free Clinic will hold open house from 3 to 8 p.m. at its new location, 5224 Lankershim Blvd., on Sunday, October 31. A Halloween theme has been set."

If you are in doubt, call the copy editor of the newspaper you are writing for. You can also pick up an inexpensive handbook on writing style at most book shops. Or you can take the easy way and leave it up to the newspaper's copy editor to correct the style.

Chapter 5

Style Manual

In writing, the word "style" has two different meanings. It may mean *the distinctive features* of literary expression that characterize a particular author. Or it may mean the opposite: *a customary manner* of presenting printed material, including usage, punctuation, spelling, typography, and arrangement. In this chapter we are using the second meaning.

FOLLOW THE STYLE OF THE NEWSPAPER

Your style must conform to that of the newspaper in which you want your story to appear. A few of the major papers in the country have their own stylebook or style sheets. If your newspaper has its own instructions on style, ask for a copy. If not, study a few editions of the paper or follow the instructions in this chapter. If the stories in the paper have a different style than this chapter, follow *their* style.

SIGNPOSTS IN WRITING

The signs that guide the reader (and the writer) through the flow of language are called marks of punctuation. Words have meaning in themselves, but punctuation helps us to find the thought contained in words as they are grouped together.

You are familiar with most of these punctuation marks. The period (.) is used to end a sentence that makes a statement. It is also used to show that a word has been abbreviated, as in Mr. or Mrs. The question mark (?) ends a sentence that asks a question. The exclamation mark (!) shows emotion, declaration, and sometimes shouting.

The comma (,) says, "Pause momentarily, then continue." It is used in addresses and dates that have two or more parts.

The semicolon (;) indicates a pause longer than that called for by a comma, but not a full stop as called for by a period. It is used to link together two or more main clauses when the writer wants to show closeness of thought between them.

The colon (:) says, "A list of items is to follow or a question is about to begin."

The apostrophe (') takes the place of a letter or letters in contracted words, as "don't"; or it shows the possessive form of nouns, as "John's guitar."

Quotation marks (" ") are used to enclose direct statements. All marks of punctuation are placed inside them when they are part of the original quotation. For example: John said, "Hand me the ball; I'm going to the field."

Single quotation marks (' ') are used to indicate a quotation within a quotation: John said, "Eddie just left. He said, 'Come to the park as soon as you can.' We should go after him."

In writing dialogue, start a new paragraph each time the speaker changes.

If a speaker talks at such length that there is more than one paragraph in the quotation, put quotation marks at the beginning of each new paragraph, but put closing quotation marks *only at the end* of the last paragraph of his remarks:

"I am going to the fair," said Doris. "You may follow me if you wish, when you are through your work.

"If Ethel comes over while I'm gone, tell her to get her own lunch. Good-bye."

HOW TO WRITE NUMERALS

Numerals can be spelled out (twenty-seven) or written as figures (7). Numerals that start a sentence *must* be spelled out.

Numbers one through nine *should* be spelled out; you may use figures for 10 and above, except with units and in certain expressions.

44

Figures should be used in matters of a statistical nature, such as time, date, age, height, weight, temperature, and score. For instance:

> "At 3 o'clock on Saturday, August 5, John Dasking, age 5, learned that he had a baby brother born the night before whose weight was 7 pounds, 4 ounces."
> "The game was played on an ideal day—temperature 78 degrees. The final score was 12 to 4."

Use figures in such expressions as 5-man team, 3-round fight, 10-gauge shotgun. But note the following: Two-way street and one-night stand.

When you have two sets of numbers together, use both figures and spelled out numerals to make it easy to understand: "There were five 4-cylinder cars, seven 6-cylinder cars, and nine 8-cylinder cars."

As in all cases of style, which style you select is not as important as being consistent within each story. And if your style is different from the newspaper, the publisher's copy editor will correct it.

USE ORDINARY SPELLING

Do not write "nite" for "night" or "thru" for "through." Editors frown on this because it distracts the attention of the reader. He reads "through" automatically and without thought; he reads, "thru" and mentally supplies the missing letters at the cost of a fraction of his attention. Avoid abbreviations except those listed in Chapter 4.

If you have difficulty with spelling, get the paperback book by Harry Shefter entitled *Six Minutes a Day to Perfect Spelling* (Washington Square Books, Dell Publishing, No. W50) or check each ambiguous word with a dictionary.

MAKE YOUR WRITING PUNCHY

Avoid adverbs. They are weak words and may weaken your writing. Instead of using an adverb to modify a verb, such as "He walked rapidly into the room," use a power verb, such as "He dashed into the room" or "He rushed into the room."

The most common offender is the word "very." The phrase "Very sincerely yours" makes one wonder what is the difference between being "very sincere" and "just a little sincere." This little verse may not be good poetry, but it will improve your writing:

Be wary Of "very."

Use power verbs when you can, and use the active form of the verb in preference to the passive form:

Passive: "An increase was reported in the cost of living during June."

Active: "The cost of living increased during June."

Use passive verbs to focus attention on the action when the actor is of no importance: "The drawbridge was lowered, and the knights rode across."

"Was lowered" is passive because it is of no importance who took this action. "Rode across" is active, focusing attention on the knights.

SENTENCE LENGTH

Sentences should vary in length, but to make your writing readable, the average number of words per sentence should be not much over 20. This means you can have long sentences—if the thought flows naturally—but they must be balanced by short sentences.

The opening sentence of an article should be short. A long sentence at the beginning may lose your reader.

Avoid using the participle form of the verb in an opening sentence:

"*Playing* an aggressive game from the first whistle, the Shortown High School basketball team *defeated* Binghampton High, their rivals for the state semifinals, 52 to 48 in the Shortown Gym and *moved* on to the finals."

The reader has to go too far to find out who is playing, and the sentence is too crowded with facts and too long for an opening sentence.

KEEP IT SIMPLE

Straightforward statements using familiar words and short sentences make clear writing. Your task as a writer is to put things into order so they can be understood by your reader. If any of his attention has to be used to decipher what you are saying, that attention is not being used to understand the subject matter.

To find out whether a sentence is simple, and therefore clear, have someone read it aloud while you listen. You can spot errors this way that do not show up when you read it silently.

BE SPECIFIC

When the Union Pacific Railroad Company was advertising for business, it used the slogan "Be specific, say Union Pacific." It is a good reminder for writers.

The opposite of "specific" is "abstract," but there are different levels of abstraction. For instance, if a shipper specified "Union Pacific" he would have been specific as far as railroad companies are concerned, but as far as trains are concerned he would have been in an intermediate level of abstraction. Let us look at several levels of abstraction about trains:

Most abstract: "Method of transportation."

Less abstract: "Trains."

Still more precise: "Union Pacific Challenger train."

More specific: "Union Pacific Challenger train leaving Los Angeles on Thursday, March 5."

It is difficult for readers to follow abstract writing because abstractions cannot be visualized—or felt or heard or smelled or touched. Specifics can be dealt with by the senses. It is easier to imagine, to visualize, to taste "a lemon pie" than to imagine, to visualize, to taste "a fancy dessert." So write about things that can be seen, felt, tasted, touched, heard, and smelled. Be specific!

STORY FORMAT

The following instructions on how to setup your story are a model as well as a manual. Follow this form:

Name of organization   FOR IMMEDIATE RELEASE
President's name, address,
   and phone
Publicity chairman's name,
   address, and phone

To make a good immediate impression, send the editor a news story that has a professional appearance. Use these instructions as a model.

Type your story double-spaced on one side only of regular $8\frac{1}{2} \times 11$ inch typewriter paper. If you don't type, get someone to type it for you. Set the left margin about 2½ inches from the edge of the paper. Also set the right margin about 2½ inches from the edge. Leave about two inches at the bottom. Paragraphs are indented four letter spaces.

Make a copy for your own files. Pica or elite type is preferred; try to avoid a script or italic font.

Type the reference data about two inches down from the upper edge on the left of the page. Include two telephone numbers so the editor can reach one or the other if he wants additional information.

Also about 2 inches from the top of the page, but at the right, type when the story is to be released. Sometimes you may need to give a specific date such as "For release: Thursday, June 10." This complicates the editor's work because he has to hold the story until that date. If it should get lost, it will not be published. It's better to send in your stories "For immediate release."

About $2\frac{1}{2}$ inches below your name start typing the body of your story. The space is for the editor. The headline and instructions to the typesetter or compositor are written there by him.

In writing letters it is correct to divide a word (between syllables) at the end of a line and to use a hyphen to show it has been divided. The purpose of this is to achieve a more nearly even right margin. A news story is different. It is written to be read by a compositor who doesn't care a thing about an even right margin in the copy. But he does find it easier not to have words divided, because then he doesn't have to decide whether to retain the hyphen. Therefore, complete the word you are typing at the end of the line, even though it may run beyond the margin.

You can type about a dozen lines on the first page. Try to end your first page in the middle of a line so it's obvious there is more. Type "more" in parentheses at the bottom of the page.

Beginning with page 2, number the pages consecutively in the upper right corner. Don't number page 1. Do not staple pages together—use a paper clip.

On following pages, 1 inch from the upper edge, type the name of the organization at the left. Then if the pages should become separated, it will be easy to identify which pages belong to your story.

Another inch below the name of the organization, continue typing the story. Type about 20 lines to the page. Counting lines is slow. You can measure 20 lines quickly by holding an $8^1{}_2 \times 11$ inch sheet of paper with 20 pretyped lines against your copy. Keep this paper on file to use for all your stories.

Be accurate. Doublecheck dates, times, places, and names. Put a little check above any unusual name to show the editor you have verified the spelling. Or you may use four or more dots under the name, in pencil, which means "let it stand."

To indicate the end of your story, type in "—30—" centered below the last line.

HOW TO KEEP YOUR STORIES BRIEF

Some publicity chairmen believe that a story that runs more than two typewritten pages is less likely to be published. But editors cannot be fooled by the following devices, so do not *crowd* your story to make it look smaller: (1) instead of typing double-spaced lines, do not set the typewriter to shift a half line when you return the carriage, (2) do not use small margins to get longer lines, and (3) do not leave too small a space above the story for the editor to write the head—leave at least 3 inches.

Do not make your story so short that it would take up less than 3 inches in the printed column. Copy less than 100 words is too small for a newspaper item—unless your publisher has an "events" section which runs small items as a kind of calendar.

If in doubt, it is better to make a story too long than too short. The editor can always cut, but he is not likely to bother to hunt up facts in order to extend a story which is too short.

FORM FOR REGULAR MEETING ANNOUNCEMENTS

Name of organization _____

Will meet at: Time_____Day and Date _____

Place _____

Purpose of meeting

Presiding officer or chairman: Name _____

Title _____

Other information

Submitted by _____
                      Name   Title

Address _____Phone _____

Mimeograph this form on paper to use for regular meeting announcements. Fill in the blank spaces and get it to the paper at least 24 hours before the deadline. The earlier the better.

Chapter 6
How To Use Photographs

Whether a picture is worth a thousand words depends on the picture, on the words, and on your purpose. There have been millions of war pictures, but is there one that can take the place of Lincoln's "Gettysburg address?"

Sometimes the picture and its caption will tell the entire story and nothing more is needed. More often—since pictures get attention quicker than words—the purpose of a picture is to catch the reader's interest and to lead him into reading your accompanying story.

Another function of pictures is to get the message published. If the editor has room for only one story and he has on his desk two stories of equal news value, one with pictures and one without, which is he going to publish? The one with pictures probably. It livens up the page and gives him a more interesting paper.

But there are good pictures and bad pictures. Maybe both stories have pictures; then the editor looks to see which picture is the most dramatic—which will catch the eye and the interest of the casual reader.

CHOOSING A SUBJECT

A good picture shows somebody doing something that tells a story. It is clear, simple, and balanced.

Who is the somebody? Well, if it really is *somebody*, a well-known VIP, people will look at the picture. A successful combination that rarely gets turned down by editors is a celebrity and members of a group doing something together and looking as though they are having fun.

If you don't have a widely known VIP, what else do readers like to look at? The most popular subjects are attractive people, babies, and animals.

ACTION

Have your subjects doing something. An honored member can be zipping up the ballerina costume which another member is donning to wear in the forthcoming dramatic production of your club. Have them talking and laughing—get them to cut loose and have fun so their faces are animated. Don't let them look at the camera; they can look at each other or at what they are doing.

If you want to add the animal theme, you can have one of the subject's pets in the picture. The animal should also be caught in a candid moment and not posed.

Or you might use the children and animals theme. A member's grandson could be hanging onto a leash which has tangled about his grandparent's legs.

THE PICTURE TELLS THE STORY

But we don't just "take a notion" to use children and animals. We build the picture so it tells the story we have to tell. If our story is about a dog show or about a benefit for a children's home, then we can use the grandson and his leash. But if the story is about a play in which a member is the star, we had better have her alone in the picture. A picture is only relevant if it tells a story.

If you can do something original—not tricky, but telling a story—it will have a better chance of being printed in a good position in the paper. If the club has decided to put on a campaign to clean up the alleys of your town, for instance, you might take a picture of the incoming officers looking over garbage and trash cans in an alley—one of them holding a trash can lid, one holding his nose, and the third holding his hands in a gesture signifying "look at this."

The caption for this picture might read:

> Surveying the trash in Danville: Newly elected officers of the Mercury Club check on the major problem their club is planning to do something about in the new

year. A double-barreled program was adopted at the Wednesday noontime luncheon meeting of the club to get owners to keep their trash in suitable containers until it is picked up, and to get the City Council to increase the pickup schedule so that trash will not be overflowing containers throughout the city. Left to right the officers-elect are Dan Jackson, president, Edward Sonehan, secretary, and James Twerman, treasurer.

Planning a photograph is like staging a play. You select the cast of characters, the costumes, the stage setting, and the props. And you pose the characters so their actions tell the story.

But that's true of everything in the picture. Each item helps tell the story. You chose it with that in mind. You chose authentic-looking costumes, an authentic-looking background, and authentic-looking props.

Some costumes, backgrounds, and props are symbols which express ideas, feelings, traditions, and much more. A judge's wig and robe are symbols of authority. A gavel is a symbol of another kind of authority. A policeman's uniform, badge, and club are symbols of a still different kind of authority.

In a photo, symbols that correspond with the theme of an event will get your idea across at a glance. If you are publicizing a fiesta, you might use a sombrero, castanets, or a serape. If it's an art auction, show an artist at his easel, wearing a smock and beret and holding a palette and brush.

Many props have been made out of cardboard or plywood. Now that Styrofoam is available, you can do magic in making props with it. To buy it, look in the yellow pages of your local phone book under the heading "Plastics—foam."

IMAGINATION UNLIMITED

With these materials you can give your imagination free play, creating oversize gadgets or miniatures. You can make a miniature house or high-rise building, or car or battleship or state capitol or dinosaur. Or you can make an oversize pair of scissors, a rabbit, spectacles, field glasses, a clock, a hat, a rifle—anything that will dramatize the idea and get across the thing you are publicizing.

Another source of props are children's toys. An adult on a kiddie car has probably been overdone, but balloons, toy wagons, dolls, and Hula-Hoops can be used in a hundred different ways. And there are many different toys.

Here's where your creativity can shine. Let your ingenious ideas for photographs show that you have imagination; that's why they made you publicity chairman. You want a photograph of the outgoing president and the new president. What symbol immediately comes to mind? A gavel. What is the most obvious idea? The outgoing president handing the gavel to the new president. It's old hat; it's been done a thousand times. So how can you vary it?

Perhaps you can pose the new president ascending the podium while the old one is stepping down. Or maybe you can show the new president addressing the group with the outgoing president in the audience.

Dig. Think. Look at gavels. Think about the president. Is there some other symbol which tells the story equally well, and which has not been used for photographs so often it is worn thin? How about showing the new president shaking hands with his predecessor while the members crowd around.

Keep on thinking. There are always new ideas. They are made by putting old things together in new ways. Get other members to help you on this. Do a little brainstorming. If you are not familiar with the process of brainstorming, look it up in the library. It's a fruitful technique of generating ideas in a group. If your members aren't familiar with it, introduce it to them. They'll find it's fun—and you'll reap a lot of ideas.

When you have chosen the idea, it will help you determine the characters you want in the picture and the props. The costumes, particularly hats, also tell a story. The stage setting, too, can help. You may not always be able to find a background that corresponds to the theme of the picture, but you can avoid those that interfere with it. Also avoid backgrounds that are so complicated or obtrusive that they create confusion in the photograph.

Whatever it is you are photographing, make a story out of it by planning ahead. Make it an action picture that tells a story.

PUTTING IT TOGETHER—COMPOSITION

Having chosen all these items, you now have to put them together. This is a matter of establishing a center of interest, relating everything in the picture to that center of interest, and choosing an appropriate setting. The setting may just be background, or it also may be a frame around your picture which holds it together.

Look for a location in which to pose your models that will afford a natural frame—archways, doors, windows, sky, or foliage. Sometimes the frame can be near the camera so the viewer is looking through a porthole, window, Christmas wreath, or doorway.

Black is beautiful. So is white. And when you have intense black beside clear white, each sharpens up the other and gives you a better picture. Contrast helps delineate things sharply and make them clear.

Other contrasts besides color will add to the impact of your picture. If you have a photo showing a little boy of 6 on the knee of his bearded grandfather of 86, the contrast emphasizes both youth and age.

Contrast can give your photographs a dramatic punch. One photographer illustrated the slogan "God is dead" with a picture of a cross sticking out of a garbage can. Contrast is good. Use it.

THREE KINDS OF PICTURES

Pictures are (1) staged, (2) on-the-spot, and (3) portraits. We have been talking about *staged* pictures. These are almost always used with advance stories and consequently are the type you will use most often. There may be half a dozen advance stories looking forward to an event, but there is usually only one cover story.

The *on-the-spot* pictures go with the cover story. These are shots taken at the masquerade ball or the fashion show. These, too, require planning, staging, and composition. Almost everything we have said about staged pictures applies also to on-the-spot pictures.

The *portrait* is a photo of a single individual—often the president of the club; sometimes a speaker or other VIP—which accompanies a story about the election of the new president or about a lecture to be delivered for the club.

Portrait photography is very different from news photography. Do not engage a portrait photographer to shoot your staged or on-the-spot pictures. Get a professional news photographer.

GETTING THE EDITOR TO SUPPLY THE PHOTOGRAPHER

The best photographer you can get is the one from the newspaper. His business is getting stories on film, just as the reporter's business is getting stories in words.

Newsworthiness is the requirement for the story in words, but with the stories on film eyecatching comes first and newsworthiness is second. The editor will assign a photographer to take your pictures if he believes you have an idea for an eyecatching picture on a newsworthy subject.

So call the editor and tell him what you have in mind. Find out when the deadline is for the paper—don't call him before the deadline; he'll be too distracted to give his best attention to your idea. Call him after the paper has been put to bed.

Some of the larger papers want requests for photographers to be made in writing, not by telephone. If that's the way they like it, that's the way you do it.

Whether you write a letter or call on the telephone, tell the editor who you are and what the event is you are publicizing. Describe briefly your idea for the picture. This means you should have thought through your idea before you phoned him. You should have kicked it about with other members of your club, going over a lot of possibilities to be sure you have come up with a real attention-getting picture. If you are telephoning, it might be well if you have a second idea to offer the editor in case he doesn't go for the first one.

This doesn't mean your first idea isn't good, but he may have something similar already scheduled. He may have some other reason for not using it. In this case offer him another good idea.

Before you phone the editor you also need to have made arrangements with the people who are to be in the picture and to know what times they could be available to be "shot." If he can't send a photographer at the times you offer, find out when his photographer can be available and check back with the subjects.

SCHEDULING

A news story can be set in type in a few minutes and fitted onto the page by the compositor, but a picture will take more time. Films have to be developed and printed, plates have to be made and mounted, and space has to be arranged. Then some big ad may crowd your picture off the page the day it is originally scheduled, and it may be a couple of days later before a space can be found for it.

If you are sending in the photo yourself, get it to the paper 10 days before it is to run. If you are going to have a staff photographer take the picture—or if you are hiring a photographer—make the arrangements two weeks ahead of the date you hope for its publication.

HANDLING PHOTOGRAPHERS

When the appointment has been made, send a note to the photographer confirming the time and the address and, if necessary, give detailed instructions on how to find you when he gets there. Include a telephone number where he can call you in case of some emergency.

Ask your people to be there 15 minutes prior to the time the picture is scheduled. You should get there before they do to see that the room is ready and that suitable dressing rooms are available for the men as well as the women. At the appropriate time, compliment them individually on how fine they look; it will help put them at ease and result in a better picture.

To be on the safe side, get a release signed by each person whose picture is taken. You can make some copies of the following form:

Photo Release

Place

For value received, I hereby grant to (your name) the right to copyright and/or publish photographs of me or photographs in which I may be included in whole or in part in conjunction with my own or a fictitious name for the purpose of illustration or any other reproduction. I hereby certify that I am over 21 years of age.

Witness   **Date**   **Signature**

Be prepared to phone anyone who does not show up on time. All those who are to be photographed should be there and ready when the photographer arrives. He may be late justifiably, since photographers are frequently assigned impossible schedules. But the paper is doing your club a favor; you are not doing it a favor—so if there is any waiting it must be your people waiting for the photographer and not him waiting for you.

Incidentally, if you want to know the cash value of the favor the paper is doing for your club, get their rate card for display advertising and figure out the value of the column inches of stories and pictures they run for you.

Be prepared to go to work immediately when the photographer arrives. When you greet him at the door, you can mention the event you are publicizing, just in case his assignment sheet may not have included this information.

People take pride in knowing how to do their job, and he will not want you telling him how to take the picture. But he will want to be informed immediately if there is some officer of your club or some other person you want to be featured in the picture. Also, if you have any props that he might want to use, he should be shown them immediately before plans for the picture begin to take shape in his mind.

NO KIBITZERS

The only people who should be present while the photographs are being taken are (1) the photographer, (2) those being photographed, and (3) you. The only exception would be someone to help with the props if they are heavy and need to be moved around.

Get rid of everybody else; or better, don't let them get there in the first place. Amateur directors do no good, and they can be a headache.

If a meeting or dance rehearsal is going on when the photographer arrives, have your arrangements made ahead of time with the subjects to follow you out to where the picture is to be taken. If the picture is to be taken on the stage where the rehearsal is in progress, make arrangements in advance with the others to go out for a coffee break, and stay out of the auditorium until you page them.

As the photographer gets the subjects posed, stand where you can see the group as the camera sees it. Have with you a clipboard with a paper on it on which you have typed up in advance what event is being publicized, the idea of the picture, and a description of the prop. Include also the name of your organization (or put this on letterhead) and your name and phone number so you can be called if more information is needed.

On this piece of paper list the names and titles or identification of the persons in the picture as they appear from left to right. A newsman will write the caption later, and if you clearly identify one of the persons as "the man with a heavy beard" it will help him to be certain he has the names connected with the right individuals.

When the photographer is through, give him this list with a smile and a word of appreciation.

The following skit may help you realize the problems a photographer has to cope with and thus enable you to cooperate with him to your mutual advantage:

PITY THE POOR PHOTOGRAPHER
A Tragedy in One Act

It's July, middle July, and it's hot. You are a news photographer with five assignments to cover in one day in Smogsville.

You arrive at your third assignment. No one is there to meet you. You hang around the building, wondering whether to go inside. You remember it's Friday... you have an early deadline, but the weekend traffic is already getting heavy. Time passes. You take out the assignment sheet: Women's Aid Society, committee for annual charity ball, the address, but no directions on how to find your people.

You walk around trying doors. You open one to peek inside the darkened room. Suddenly there's a Doberman pinscher guard dog challenging your kneecap.

Your women arrive, breathlessly complaining of the traffic and the heat. They are dressed all in black and carry big, bulky props. They ask you where Thelma is. Quickly you deduce that Thelma isn't the Doberman. She must be the missing publicity chairman who made these arrangements. You put her on your list.

"Doesn't know her public relations work.

You start without her, or try to. How do you break up all that heavy-looking black?

"Ladies, please stand over here."

"No, maybe you better sit over there; uh, better yet, some of you sit and one stand."

"Mrs. Hutsenfutz, will you put your cigarette down?"

"Now for a big smile and .. NO! The Doberman doesn't fit in the picture. Cute? Ummmmnnn ... yes. Please ladies, I have to be across town in 15 minutes. Just smile, please."

You're in focus and ready to shoot. Suddenly they are all lined up in a row, staring self-consciously straight into the camera. While redirecting them, you look around for a telephone to call your next assignment to say you've been delayed. Thelma arrives in a flurry of curls and eyelashes that sparkle.

You take her off your list and put her in the picture. You make her the center of interest. She has on black and white which draws the eye. You shoot the picture.

While you are trying to get the names and titles down correctly from left to right, you spot a telephone, but the Doberman is guarding it. While you're hassling him to get to the phone, the ladies leave. When you return to ask Thelma for the names, she has forgotten the name of the president and founder of her group.

"We always call her Dodo," she apologizes.

You write, "Left to right, Mrs. Dodo Head, president, etc." and hit the freeway, an hour late for your next assignment.

Moral: Several different morals may be derived from this tale. You write in the one that seems most appropriate.

GETTING A PHOTOGRAPHER

If the newspaper cannot supply a photographer, your next best thing is to employ a professional news photographer.

Billy Jones may have a camera and the time, but without experience in news photography he may become so self-conscious when confronted with an important person that the photograph he gets is a picture of his shoelaces.

If you can't employ a professional news photographer, you may have to take the pictures yourself. If you do, keep the following things in mind.

SHOOTING THE PICTURE

The center of interest should not be in the exact center of your picture. Shoot so that it is a little to one side an a little above or below the center. Everything in the picture should draw the viewer's attention to the center of interest. The characters can be pointing at it, looking at it, reaching for it, holding it, surrounding it, or laughing at it. If the center of interest is a person, the others can be giving him their attention, cheering him, smiling at him, or handing things to him—the possibilities are limitless.

Note that there should not be more than three others. Four people are maximum in a picture; two or three are better. And keep them close together.

Some people get uptight when a camera is pointed at them. So get your camera focused so you can forget it while you direct them. People feel more relaxed when they are doing things; so tell them what to do, and get them to play the role, ham it up, laugh, and come to life. Then snap several shots while you keep talking to them and directing their attention to what they are doing. Get them to talk back to you (without looking at you) and to talk to each other.

Professional photographers take lots of shots—then they select the good ones. Follow their example: if you are going to want 2 pictures, take 20. To save money, don't have them all printed. When they are developed, you can look at the negatives—or at sheet proofs. From these you can select the ones you want to use and have them printed.

Most newspapers prefer 8×10 inch glossy prints. Some want 5×7 inches or some other size. Find out what size the editor wants, and get your prints that size. But usually any size black and white glossy print with good contrast will do. Do not use color film unless your photo is going to be used in a color supplement. Make sure you ask whoever develops your prints for a *glossy print*, not a textured one.

WRITING CAPTIONS

Words can tell a story without pictures, but very few pictures can get the message across without some accompanying words to explain what they're all about. These words form the caption.

If the pictures are taken by a staff photographer from the newspaper, give him the list of names and titles of the people in the photographs and a "suggested caption." A writer at the paper will probably rewrite it.

But if you are supplying the pictures to the paper, you will have to supply captions with them. The caption should be brief—two or three lines are best. Study the captions of pictures in the paper to which you are submitting and model yours after them.

You will observe that, like the pictures themselves, some captions are better than others. The striking caption is usually one with an imaginative idea about what the people are doing expressed in the first few words. Following that should be plain and simple information as to what the picture is and who the people are.

When you come to write a caption, *look* at the picture. Imagine yourself a stranger who has no idea what it is about. What are the things you want to know about it? Use your checklist for news: who, what, where, when, why, and how?

The "who" comes first in this list because it is the most important. Editors and readers resent captions that do not clearly identify the people in the picture. Do not list them in the order of their importance. List them as they appear in the picture. Begin with the person on the left, and identify each one in order from left to right. For example:

"Left to right, back row: Mr. and Mrs. John S. Sanders, Miss Estelle Smith, treasurer, and Mrs. Ethel Vandenburg; front row: Mrs. Smith Jones and Miss Evelyn Greer, president of Philopean Society."

TYPING AND PASTING

When you get a satisfactory caption, type it on a plain white paper cut to the width of the photograph. Leave a 3-inch margin at the top and double space your typing.

Spread paste 1 inch wide on the upper edge. Attach the sheet of paper to the *bottom back* of the photograph so that at one glance you can see the picture and the caption below it. Clip the unit to a piece of cardboard. Put the name of your organization on the back of the photograph *lightly* in pencil.

HANDLING AND MAILING

Handle all photos, prints, and negatives by their edges to avoid fingerprints on the finish. Do not type or write hard on back. Do not attach anything to them with staples or paper clips. Store them in a mailing envelope with plenty of cardboard to keep them flat.

Sometimes the photograph is smaller than the envelope, and if the cardboard is the same size as the picture it may slip around inside the envelope so as to leave the photo without protection. To avoid this, cut another piece of cardboard nearly the same size as the envelope to give the whole package protection.

Instead of cardboard, maybe you would rather use vinyl plastic report covers. Take a look at them when you are in the stationery store. They, too, should fit the envelope snugly so the photograph can't be damaged.

LEFTOVER PHOTOGRAPHS

Use leftover photographs on posters. Enlargements of photographs the newspaper doesn't run can be mounted on posters and bulletin boards with the same caption you have writter for the paper—or even a longer caption and story.

Keep a record of pictures and stories. Use 3 × 5 inch file cards. Head each card with a caption. Enter the name of the publication, the date sent out, and the date of publication.

Enter the information at the proper time and every time. Don't depend on memory.

Chapter 7
How To Get
Your Stories Published

If you are tempted to contact the editor to introduce yourself and have a brief chat with him, the best advice is "don't." Your contacts with him—at least in the beginning—should be through your news releases. If they are brief and well written he will appreciate you. Your phone number is on your releases; if the editor wants to talk with you, let him take the initiative.

If you want to know what the newspaper's deadline is for your kind of stories, of course you may ask. But ask the editor's secretary or someone else on the staff. Try not to bother the editor.

If you live in a suburban or rural community, your newspaper probably has a local correspondent covering your town. Usually the newspaper will print the name and phone number of the local reporter at least once a week. If there is such a person assigned to your town, dial him directly and forget the editor.

MAKING FRIENDS WITH THE EDITOR

The best way to make friends with the editor is to not bother him. Believe it or not, he's busier than you are. He has far more to do than he can get done, and if you take up his time—even just a few minutes of his time—you are a distraction keeping him from getting at some of those things.

If you believe that a little apple polishing is a good thing, you're right. But the important word in that sentence is "little." If you can't resist the temptation to make the acquaintance of the editor, pop in on him (after the paper has been "put to bed") just long enough to introduce yourself and tell him what a fine paper he is publishing. Tell him you know he is busy; wish him well and say goodbye. He'll love you—not so much for coming in as for understanding how busy he is and for not wasting his time.

Don't even do this until after you have sent him several stories and at least one has been published (which you can thank him for) so that when you do come in and introduce yourself as publicity chairman of the Coordinating Council for Survival Research he will be able to identify you and say (to himself, if not to you), "Oh, yes. This is the person who sends in those professional-looking, brief, and to-the-point news releases."

Chapter 1 contains the quotation "Nothing on earth will cause men to work so long or so hard as will sincere appreciation." Napoleon Hill's magazine once carried an editorial about this, stating that the most important word in that sentence is the word "sincere." You can apply this to your job. The best apple polishing might be to send the editor a letter on club stationery as follows:

Dear Mr. Roberts:

Thank you for publishing the story about our charity ball. You helped make it a success, and we turned in $183.25 to the Boy's Club of Formerstone.

Sincerely yours,

NEVER PUT AN EDITOR ON THE SPOT

One thing you should never do is to ask an edior why your story wasn't published. To ask such a question seems to imply that you think you have a right to have your story published, and if it isn't in the paper it is his responsibility to explain why.

There may be no good reason why your story wasn't published. As was explained in the third chapter, every newspaper receives far more stories than there is space for. Some of them can't be printed just because of lack of space. You can't win 'em all. If your last story didn't get published, write the best story you can next time. Persistence will pay off.

On the other hand. there may be a very good reason why your story didn't appear. If there is a reason, you probably can find it in this book—and by looking at the smallest stories buried in the back pages of the paper. Study them until you understand why they got in the paper and yours didn't.

If you are dealing with a local correspondent. your chances of getting your story published are good. This person is usually paid for all news printed about the town he covers. and he will be glad to get material.

WHY THE WASTEBASKET?

A noted professional publicity director once said. "The amount of money wasted on paper. envelopes. and stamps in sending stacks of release to newspapers of this country is appalling when so much of it ends up in the wastebasket."

Why does it end up in the wastebasket? The most common reason is that the story will not interest enough of the readers of the paper. It's the business of an editor to know what his readers want to read. and you must know. too.

If an editor has two stories of equal interest and only room for one. the one that will end up in the wastebasket is the one which is poorly written. If you follow the instructions in Chapter 3. there need be nothing wrong with your stories. If they are newsworthly. short. and well-written. what else can you do to help get more of them published? Several things ...

GETTING STORIES PUBLISHED

1. *Get your stories to the newspapers in time.*

   A story that comes in after the deadline is likely to have three strikes against it—it's out. Similarly. a story that comes in too far ahead of the publishing date has two strikes against it. It is not convenient for an editor to hold a story that comes in ahead of time. Send your story in at the right time marked "For immediate release."

   Timing for photogaphs is different; see Chapter 6.
2. *Avoid Duplication.*

   The editor will get confused if two persons from the same organization presume to speak for it. It's like listening to two stations at once on the radio. Sharp tuning is essential for a clear message. See to it that no other person tries to speak for your organization. The only exception to this—repeat, only—is when the newspaper tries to reach you and can't. Then they call the president, whose name and phone number are along with yours on the news release.

3. *Give the editor a roster of your members.*

   Find out which editor handles the material for your organization, and see that he or she has an up-to-date roster.

4. *Monday is a good day.*

   With most daily newspapers, Monday is the day when advertising and news are light. Check to find out when is the best time to deliver a story for Monday's paper.

5. *Invite a reporter to your event.*

   If you are having a dinner or a fashion show, better than sending tickets is to deliver them in person. Make a point of finding out ahead of time the name of the reporter or editor who is coming. When he arrives, roll out the red carpet. Confirm his name and call him by name, introduce him to the VIPs, and have a seat reserved for him. Hand him a "fact sheet" containing the names of the people involved and all other essential data that he will need in writing the story. After the event, send him a "thank you" note.

6. *Consider an advertising contract.*

   Some newspapers run a church page, a real estate section, an automobile section, and other special sections. The stories therein are largely written by advertising agencies and publicists handling the accounts of the advertisers. Hardly anyone is surprised if the stories in a special section are about the firms that are advertised in that section.

   The editorial department must correlate its work with the advertising department regarding space, since the amount of advertising sold for the day generally determines the number of pages in the paper and, to some degree, how many columns an editor will have for news.

   Nevertheless, the editorial department will claim there is no connection between the stories run and the ads you place with the paper. They strive to see to it that the news is news. published on its own merit and not because somebody has bought an ad in the paper. They do not want the paper to become a "puff sheet" for advertisers. Consequently, you will have to decide for yourself whether it would help you get stories published if you were to sign a contract for a 1 or 2 inch display ad each week.

7. *Cover the papers others overlook.*

Find out what foreign language newspapers circulate in your area. These would be especially good outlets for a story about a member of your club affiliated with the national group the paper caters to. Learn also about college newspapers. underground publications. and labor union papers.

House organs or newsletters of other organizations also may be places where a story can be run on special occasions. Build up a list of these offbeat story outlets that the average publicity chairman is likely to overlook.

8. *Fix in your mind that there is no such thing as a "throw away" paper.*

Those newspapers you find on your doorstep carrying the ads of the weekend specials for the local stores are "free distribution newspapers." If you ever refer to one as a "throw away sheet" you may mortally wound the editor. and this might be fatal to your relationship with him.

9. *Don't phone it: write it.*

The only time you can phone a story to a newspaper is when you have a really big story that breaks just at the deadline. It's got to be really big. All other stories should be written.

Chapter 8

How To

Use Radio and TV

Everyone realizes you can reach a lot of people with a message over radio or TV. So nearly everyone (it seems to the station manager) wants to have his message broadcast. Unfortunately, most of the air time must be sold to pay the costs of keeping the station operating, and there is not enough time left to broadcast all the public service announcements. Most of them cannot be aired. Your goal is to see that your message is one of the fortunate few that do get on the air. This chapter tells you how.

PUBLIC SERVICE ANNOUNCEMENTS

PSA stands for public service announcement. Stations need to broadcast a reasonable number of public service announcements to retain their licenses. Once in a while someone thinks he has a right to time on the air, and he demands it. This merely antagonizes the station personnel.

You don't get time on the air by demanding it. Your program must be "sold" to the radio or TV station on its merits. Since the station has lots more public service announcements than it has time, the program director has to choose which ones to put on and which ones to omit. The person who tries to demand time on the air is almost certain to be omitted.

HOW TO GET YOUR MESSAGE BROADCAST

Getting the station to air your message is a specific application of the general principle mentioned in Chapter 1: the way to get what you want from other people is to give them what they want.

The way to get your message broadcast is to supply the station with a message that people will want to hear, fitted to their time slots, and in the form that they can use.

Which people? There are different audiences. A radio station specializing in classical music has a different audience than a station given over to rock.

Each station will select for presentation those programs which will interest its listeners. Therefore the first thing you must do is to monitor the programs and determine the kind of audience the station is reaching. Then tailor your pitch to that audience.

There are also different typs of programs that you might participate in and different types of announcements:

1. *Station breaks*. These occur during a network program to give the local station the opportunity to identify itself by its call letters and to make a brief pitch. Usually the time has been sold to an advertiser, but if it has not the station may use a public service spot. Be sure it has some of yours on hand—15 to 20 words. Written copy required.

2. *Spot announcements*. These run 10, 20, 30, or 60 seconds. They make a single point. A "personality spot" is made by a celebrity. Usual opening: "This is Josh Morgan inviting you to ... "

3. *News release*. Stations have an almost unlimited amount of news coming over the ticker tape. To get your story on the air in competition with this, it must be really newsworthy for the local audience. Human interest items about local people have a good chance of being aired. Write it as briefly as possible. Pack in the who, what, when, where, why, and how without an excess word. And get it to the station *right now* while it is still news.

4. *Community calendar*. Some stations group together announcements of events and activities in the area, calling this part of their program "Community

Bulletin Board" or "Calendar Announcements" or some similar title. Written copy is required.

5. *Two-way radio.* Also called "Telephone Talk Shows" or "Open Mike Programs" in chich listeners phone in and "spout off" comments which are heard over the air. Because lots of people are trying to phone in, the lines are usually busy and it is difficult to break through. By having a number of the members of your organization trying to dial the program, you may be fortunate enough to have one get on the air. Each of them should be prepared with a sheet of information which will help them get the message across and generated as much discussion of it as possible.

6. *Editorials.* Some stations present their editorial viewpoint on community and national events. A common practice is to grant equal time to qualified individuals or organizations with a different point of view. However. there is no law requiring them to give time to your group. or any specific group. So do not "demand" time to answer one of their editorials. Instead. "offer" them a different point of view.

Sometimes you can offer them what appears to be a rebuttal. which doesn't actually deny or refute what they have said. but which presents a quite different idea about the subject.

A certain amount of controversy will build the station's audience. and the station manager likes this. But controversy must be rapid fire. The riposte should be on the air as soon as possible after the thrust. So contact the station immediately when you hear its editorial to offer your rebuttal. If the station wants to use it. it will likely schedule it as soon as you can get it ready.

7. *Features.* If one of the stations in your area presents features. that is. short presentations of community programs and items of interest. you may be able to have one of the activities of your organization used as the subject.

"One of the activities" does not mean the organization itself. An organization is not a suitable subject—organizations are static. The audience wants action and conflict. Drama is conflict.

Furthermore, in any story—of an individual or of an activity—success is not interesting by itself. It is appreciated only when it is the outcome of a struggle; the more difficult the struggle, the greater the audience involvement. Audiences are held by conflict, difficulty, threat, and the danger of failure.

Therefore show the purpose of the activity, and the obstacles that had to be overcome before its purpose could be achieved. Show the attempts that failed, the difficulties, the trouble—and how the people involved are coping and succeeding.

To present the idea for the program to the station, prepare fact sheets giving all pertinent information.

8. *Panel discussion programs.* A regular panel program needs fresh participants each time it goes on the air. If you can suggest to the producer or the master of ceremonies a good person for his panel, he will appreciate it.

You can also suggest topics related to your organization, and possible panel guests from your organization who could present viewpoints of interest to the audience.

Topics for panel programs get to an audience for the same reasons that feature programs get to them. So in proposing the program to the station, follow the previous instructions for features. Follow this formula: purpose, conflict, crisis (where it appears that all is lost), and then (presto!) success.

Prepare fact sheets giving the answers to all the questions the producer of the show may ask.

Incidentally, do not attempt to produce your own panel program. Get on an established program which has already built up its audience, developed a successful format, and worked the bugs out and has experienced personnel.

9. *Interviews.* The broadcaster who uses interviews will be glad to have you supply a competent VIP for the program. Note the word "competent." Be sure the individual to be interviewed has had experience in front of a mike. Show the station background material on the person you are offering.

A caution with this type of program: Some interviewers specialize in controversy, even to the point of antagonizing and upsetting the participant. Avoid getting into a situation where ill will may be created, either with the guest or with the audience.

10. *Speeches*. We don't call them "speeches" because the audience has a negative reaction to the word. We call them "personal appearances."

When you have an event planned at which you will have a name speaker—we call him "a celebrity"—contact the station personnel well in advance and let them know you have a subject of interest to their audience.

If they want to present him, the speech will need to be typed out with extra copies for the station. Provide biographical data for the announcer to use in introducing him. Indicate his relation to your organization.

11. *Canned programs*. Recorded, taped, or filmed programs have several advantages. They can be made at the most convenient time and broadcast later. They can be used over and over. And they can be edited and thus improved.

If your group is part of a national organization, the national office may supply taped programs you can use on radio and also on TV. Work out with the program director of the station which of these he can use.

GETTING ACQUAINTED

When you have monitored the station and ascertained the type of audience it reaches and which programs you might fit into, the next thing to do is to get acquainted.

Telephone the program director, introduce yourself and your organization, and ask for an appointment to discuss public service time and the types of programming he would like you to supply. Incidentally, when the appointment has been arranged, get there a little early. Television and radio people have a tight schedule; they cannot wait for anyone. Therefore, when the time comes be there waiting for him.

KNOW WHAT YOU'RE DOING

Before you go—before you even call for an appointment—know what you are doing. Imagine how the program director feels when someone comes in and says, "we would like some publicity on public service time."

"For what?" he asks.

"For the Eddie Glutz Boys Club."

"Well, what are you doing? What event is there to publicize?"

"We don't have any special thing in mind at the moment, but there are activities throughout the year."

The director is probably thinking about a program that has to go on the air in an hour, and the recordings haven't arrived yet. He must get on the phone and find out where they are. Perhaps he will have to create a substitute program. He needs to get at it.

He is going to say, "Fine. When you have some activity coming up that you want to announce, come back and tell me about it. It has been a pleasure meeting you, and I wish the Eddie Glutz Club success. Good day."

When you have an appointment with a program director have definite things in mind. What do you want to publicize? What is your basic idea? What is your message? Who is interested in it? Why? How can it be gotten across to them? You should have several possible answers to this last question. This is part of what you came to talk with him about. Have several alternative proposals to present.

If your club is celebrating an anniversary or has a member with an unusual record of service or is planning to expand, inquire whether the station would be interested in programs using these items as a base.

FIT THE PROGRAM TO THE STATION

Try to keep the proposals appropriate to the material. If a few spot announcements will do it, don't suggest a 15 minute speech.

When you make suggestions to the program director for programs on his station, be sure you have done your homework. You'll really cut off your welcome if you offer him a suggestion for a panel program and it turns out that particular program is broadcast each week over a competing station.

BE PREPARED

Know his station; know all you can about it; know its programs. Have a file on it with as much information as you can gather: names of its officers and staff—manager, program director, announcers, disc jockeys, news editors, commentators, and special program personalities. Study its programs carefully, and have information on them in your file. Follow the station in the radio-TV guide, and in the newspaper radio-TV section. When you go to talk with the program director—or anyone at the station—practice the Boy Scout motto: "Be prepared."

Part of your preparation should be the creation of a file of the people who are available to help with radio and TV programs. List members or friends in the broadcasting industry who can write continuity or scripts for programs, speakers who are good at repartee for interview programs, and those who are good on panels with these areas of expertise.

Perhaps you can get members of your club who will monitor certain stations for you and follow their programs and give you notes, suggestions, and various aids in dealing with each station in your area. You can then consult with these members about programs or announcements before you offer them to the station. These monitors can be your "radio-TV committee" along with others who can be helpful.

TRY A DIFFERENT VIEWPOINT

In preparing for your interview, try a different viewpoint. Instead of asking yourself "What can this station do for us?" Work on the question "What can we do for the station?" Ask yourself "What does the station need?" Decide which of the programs you can offer will best serve its interests.

When you talk with the program director, if you can offer him something to help his programming you will distinguish yourself in his mind from the people who come in just to get something. If you can think as he thinks, you will find beautiful cooperation.

The station wants (1) listeners, (2) programs that will attract listeners, (3) freedom from trouble, and (4) appreciation. You can help with each of these things.

1. *Listeners*. When the station puts on a program for your organization, advertise it, publicize it, and get people to listen to it. Announce it in your newsletter and at your meetings, and get your members to listen. Have them get their friends and neighbors to listen. Put up posters about it.

Send a story about it to the newspaper. Perhaps you can take an ad in the paper announcing the program. Maybe you can send out a special mailing about it. Send copies of these things to the station manager, program director, and anyone else who might be interested so they will know how hard you are working to build an audience for their station.

2. *Programs that will attract listeners.* If you have a celebrity in your membership who would be willing to make a radio or TV appearance, let the program director know. First be sure you have the cooperation of the celebrity.

If you have a name speaker coming, let the station know well in advance.

If yours is a chapter of a national organization, you may be able to offer the station programs that originate in the national office. These are likely to be of high quality, and the station will be glad to know that they are available.

Any other program you offer them should be checked to be sure it is one that will attract listeners.

3. *Freedom from trouble.* The purpose of this chapter is not to make you an expert in radio and TV broadcasting but to help you work *with* the experts. The more you know about the broadcasting business, the more helpful you can be—or perhaps it is more to the point to say the less you will get in their hair. The complete amateur who makes insane suggestions or who wants impossible things is the person they want to avoid. Your job, in part, is to keep them happy about the things the station does for you.

4. *Appreciation.* A note of thanks should be sent afterward, of course. But more than that, see that letters are sent to the station from people who heard the program, commending the station on it. This evidence of audience interest is of tremendous importance.

This is not vanity on the part of the station, it's a fact of business. Letters indicating the extent of listener interest in the programs are a basis for selling advertising, which is the source of the money necessary to operate the station.

Furthermore, stations can broadcast only if they have a license from the Federal Communications Commission. These licenses are issued for a period of three years and have to be renewed periodically. When the license comes up for renewal, the station needs to show that it has been doing a substantial amount of public service. Your letters of appreciation are evidence it can submit to the FCC. Consequently, they are vital to the station.

PROFESSIONAL-LOOKING COPY

It is important that you present professional-looking copy. Pages that contain typos, deletions, misspellings and that are, in general, hard to read will more than likely be rejected. The following are some rules for presenting professional-looking copy.

1. *Format.* Typewrite all copy, double-spaced on letter size (8½ × 11 inch) bond paper. Do not use onion skin which rattles and can be heard over the air when pages are turned. Leave a margin of 2 inches on the left and on the right. Six lines from the upper edge on the left side put the name of your organization and your name, address, and phone number. On the right put the date or dates when the material is to be used. (See the models that follow later in this chapter.)

   One-third of the way down the page start typing copy. Indent paragraphs four spaces. Do not hypenate a word at the end of a line; write out the full word. Do not complete a paragraph at the bottom of a page; break it in two, and put the balance of it on the next page.

   Usually stations want two copies, but check with the station to which you are submitting. It may want more. Use sharp carbon to be sure all copies are completely legible.

2. *Content.* If you are writing a news story, follow the instructions in Chapter 3. Use tight writing with not an excess word. Check your "six honest serving-men."

   If you are writing announcements, count the words to fit the time: 25 words for 10 seconds, 50 words for 20 seconds, and 150 words for 60 seconds. Each digit in a number counts as one word.

Make a single point—just one—per announcement. Tell the listener exactly what you want him to know or to do. Read your copy aloud to check the way it sounds and to time it. Indicate the reading time on the copy.

If there could be any possible question as to the way to pronounce a name. give phonetic spelling in parenthesis immediately following the name. for example. von Hunze (vahn Hun-zee).

The program director has to plan schedules well in advance so they can be published in radio-TV magazine directories and in newspapers. To make it easy for him to work your material in, submit program copy 10 days in advance and news stories a week or more in advance.

BROADCASTING OR RECORDING

When broadcasting live or making a recording for radio, the first rule is *be on time*. To be sure about this. get there a little ahead of time.

You will be given instructions as to the correct distance between your mouth and the microphone. Incidentally, if you talk across the mike instead of directly into it. the sibilants (the hissing in the voice) will be less noticeable.

When a speaker on the air finishes one sheet of his notes. if he turns the paper over it may make a noise that can be heard by the listeners. Therefore do not turn your sheets of paper over: slide them to one side silently.

TV is more expensive than radio. makes a greater impact, and requires more preparation. Get expert counsel to help you prepare TV programs—someone from the production end of TV. not from the business office.

You will need to monitor the programs, just as for radio, but you will have to pay attention to the visual material used in the commercials since this is what you will have to supply to the station.

Sound-on-film has the advantage that the station can use it even without an announcer on duty. Slides. flip cards. or photos are second best with an announcer's voice reading the copy. Slides are 16 mm or 35 mm transparencies. Find out which size is used by the station you are dealing with, and supply them with the size they want.

Stations greatly prefer slides to flip cards or photos. Therefore. give them slides and you will have a better chance of having your announcement broadcast. They are inexpensive. The station will tell you who makes them locally.

If for some reason you cannot get a slide made of a photo and must use the photo, get a dull-finish print since glossy prints reflect the lights.

You will need one slide, card, or photo for each 10 seconds of copy. Be sure the picture is related to the copy. Let the station put its own identifying number on the slide.

TV copy is not read as rapidly as radio copy. For TV write 20 words for 10 seconds, 40 words for 20 seconds, and 125 words for 60 seconds.

Some TV stations may be able to use colored slides; others may not. To find out things like this, contact the promotion director or the public affairs director, if the station has one, and ask what the requirements are and how you can best fit the methods of operation.

If yours is a national organization, your national office may have already sent material directly to the station. If so, find out about it and cooperate in whatever way you can.

The station may have a tray of stock PSA slides. You can look through this and select slides that would be suitable for your announcement—or write an announcement fitted to the available slides. In the process you may find material which is outdated and should be discarded and replaced.

If you want your visual material returned, be sure to let the station know. Otherwise it may get thrown away.

PERSONAL APPEARANCES

TV appearances may be live or taped. Keep clothes simple. Soft, medium colors or pastels are good for women. Men should not wear white shirts. Avoid sharply contrasting colors and patterns. Avoid heavy makeup. Don't wear noisy bracelets or sparkling or bright metal jewelry.

If you normally wear glasses, use them so you can see the director and floor manager during your appearance. They may want to give you hand signals while you are on.

FOLLOW-THROUGH

As in tennis and golf, it's the follow-through that puts the winning touch on your work. With radio and TV this has two parts: letters to the station and keeping your announcements up-to-date.

As mentioned before, letters of two kinds should be sent: your letter expressing appreciation for the program or for broadcasting your spot announcements, and letters from your members written not as members of the organization but just as listeners to the station. These should be straight fan letters telling how much they enjoyed the program.

The other kind of follow-through has to do with your spot and other announcements. When you sent them in, you indicated that they were to be used between certain dates. When those dates are past, the station will throw the announcements away.

Keep a schedule showing what announcements are with which stations so that when the period of their use expires you can get new announcements to them. You also need this record to be sure you do not send announcements to a station which pile on top of other announcements you have sent them, indicating to them that you don't know what you are doing. Keep the follow-through organized.

FOR FURTHER READING

The National Association of Broadcasters issues a free booklet entitled *If You Want Air Time*. Ask your local radio or TV station for a copy.

The National Public Relations Council publishes a booklet by Roy E. Johnson entitled *Making the Most of Radio-TV*. Try your local bookstore for this publication.

SAMPLE 10 SECOND SPOT RADIO ANNOUNCEMENT

From: For use:

Parents/Students/Teachers for Free Education
                                        Wednesday, April 7
Gerald Freeman, Publicity Director
132 Sixth Street   through
Wilburforce, Ohio
Phone: Failure 2-6336   Thursday, April 22

   TIME: 10 seconds

   WORDS: 28

   ANNCR: "Schools are jails," says Yvonne Ellis, who will
        speak Friday evening, Community Auditorium, 2010
        Main Street. Subject: "Repeal the Compulsory School
        Attendance Law." Free admission.

SAMPLE 20 SECOND SPOT RADIO ANNOUNCEMENT

From: For use:

Operation Survival (Q)   Monday, March 5
Morgan Montgomery
Publicity Chairman   through
3959 Shedd Terrace   Tuesday, March 20
Culver City, California 90230
(213) 870-6286

TIME: 20 seconds
WORDS: 53

ANNCR: Survival is all that matters today. Unless people
control the bomb, population, and pollution, the entire
human race will die. There will be no one left on earth.
Effort devoted to any other problem will have been
wasted. Write for free booklet "Operation Survival,"
3959 Shedd Terrace, Culver City, California.

SAMPLE NEWS RELEASE FOR RADIO OR TV

From: For immediate release

Federal Union, Inc.
John Boland,
Public Information Officer
1736 Columbia Road, N.W.
Washington, D.C. 20009
Phone: (202) 234-2211

A free booklet, "It's Time to Merge!" is offered by Federal Union, an organization of public spirited citizens who believe that not enough is being done to keep peace and prevent depression.

Clarence Streit, president of Federal Union and editor of the international monthly *Freedom & Union*, says that a federation of the free nations is the best guarantee of peace. His organization believes that such a federation could grow gradually until it includes all nations in a peaceful, cooperative commonwealth.

This booklet is a capsule summary of how this could be brought about. It consists mostly of cartoons by Channing L. Bete. The first page says, "Don't read this booklet if you are happy with the world as it is."

But if you are not happy with the world as it is and want to know what can be done to improve things, you can get a free copy of "It's Time to Merge!" by writing Federal Union, 1736 Columbia Road, N.W., Washington, D. C. 20009.

(END)

TV News Editor Note: Enclosed photo of Clarence Streit and copy of booklet "It's Time to Merge!"

SAMPLE 10 SECOND SPOT TV ANNOUNCEMENT

From: For use:

Survival Research   March 1
Mark Lyman. Educational Director
P. O. Box 91591   through
Los Angeles 90009   March 20
Phone: 870-6286

    TIME: 10 Seconds
               AUDIO
    VIDEO
        Slide No.____(girl
        holding globe of
        earth. March 21
        calendar in back-
        ground)
        ANNCR: Your planet needs your planning. On
    Earth Day. March 21, plan activities for this
    year to beautify the earth.

(Note: The blank in "Slide No._____" is for the station
to insert its own identifying number of your slide.)

SAMPLE 20 SECOND SPOT TV ANNOUNCEMENT

From: For use:

Santa Monica Consumers Cooperative Society   October 1
Edgar Winston,
Public Information Chairman   through
2021 Barrington Avenue   October 20
Los Angeles 90025
Phone: 478-0221

TIME: 20 seconds
          AUDIO
VIDEO
    Slide No.   (man
    paying bill on leav-
    ing garage)

    Slide   No.   (same
    man, car on tow
    truck   car   hoist
    heading into gar-
    age; owner point-
    ing to sign "Under
    New   Manage-
    ment")

ANNCR: Is Nader right? Does big business
    pollute the world, exploit the consumer, cor-
    rupt the government? Hear Dalton Masters
    tell "How Consumer CO-ops Succeed Where
    Government Regulation Fails." CO-op Com-
    munity Room, 2021 Barrington, Friday, Oc-
    tober 20, 8:30. Free admission.

SAMPLE 60 SECOND SPOT TV ANNOUNCEMENT

From: For use:

Coordinating Council for   Thursday, November 1
Survival Research and Education
Mark Lyman. Educational Director   through
P. O. Box 91591   Wednesday, November 14
Los Angeles 90009
Phone: 870-6286

                                        TIME: 60 seconds
VIDEO   AUDIO

Slide No. (booklet) ANNCR:	The Coordinating Council for Survival Research and Education offers a free booklet. "The Earth Looks Beautiful from Outer Space."
Slide No. (riots and pollution)	<u>Standing on the surface and looking about the</u> world. one sees war. poverty. pollution. riots. hunger.
Slide No. (photo of earth from outer space)	But from outer space. where the earth is seen as a whole. it looks beautiful. Most major problems arise because people have not dealt with the earth as a whole.
Slide No. (globe with nations in different colors)	Instead of organizing this planet for efficient administration of its resources. people have marked off artificial boundaries and are spending fortunes and sacrificing their own children to maintain them.
Slide No. (geographical globe. no national boundaries)	This booklet shows how earth could be administered as a beautiful home for all.
Super Slide No. (address)	For free copy write Survival Research. Box 91591. Los Angeles 90009

(Note: "Super" means superimpose a slide—on clear glass—
over the previous slide.)

Chapter 9

Your Public Image

If you have ever had the experience of waiting for a friend to come walking down the street, you probably thought you saw him coming several times only to find when the person got close enough that it wasn't your friend at all. Because you were looking for your friend you "saw" him even when it wasn't really him. We tend to see that which we are looking for—the image we have in our minds.

PEOPLE SEE WHAT THEY EXPECT TO SEE

This is the basis of the creation of a public image. People are given an interpretation of facts; they are told what they are going to see, so that's what they see.

When P. T. Barnum merged the Barnum & Bailey Circus with the Ringling Brothers Circus, he advertised his performances as "The Greatest Show on Earth." And when people came away from that circus they had seen the greatest show on earth. Why? Because that's what they had been told they were going to see. Barnum had established a certain image in the minds of people, and when they looked they saw the image they had in their minds.

YOUR CREATIVE ROLE

The same thing will happen with your club or organization. People will tend to see the image you put in their minds. This is its public image. You create it. But first you must have it in your mind. What kind of an organization is it? What kind of an organization do you want it to be?

Your work as publicity chairman will do more than almost anything else to create the public image of your club. And the club, in turn, will tend to live up to the image of it that its members and the public have in their minds.

YOUR ORGANIZATION'S BROCHURE

A good many organizations have a basic brochure or fact sheet which sets forth the purpose of the organization, its program, its history, what it is today, who its members are, and how to join (if membership is open). If you have inherited such a statement, look it over critically and creatively along with the other officers and ask whether it is adequate. Does it present the picture of the organization that you and the officers have in mind and that you want the public to have in mind? If not, rewrite it.

If your group does not already have a basic statement of this kind, prepare one. You can think of many uses for it, but you will find that it is also helpful in numerous situations which you do not anticipate.

A sample page from a brochure is illustrated here. Get others from your chamber of commerce, local clubs, and community groups—ask your members to save you those they receive in the mail from national organizations. From all these sources you can get good ideas which you can adapt to your own club.

THE PROGRAM OF FRIENDS OF ANIMALS, INC.

Education. Our campaign against the accidental and amateur breeding of pets appears in pamphlets, magazines, newspapers, on radio and television.

Financial Assistance. Friends of Animals, Inc., gives financial help to those who cannot afford prevailing fees for spaying. The medium for this help is a subsidized spaying certificate that guarantees fair payment to any registered veterinarian. The amount of the subsidy in the individual case depends on our funds and the applicant's need.

Aid to Animal Shelters. All humane societies and dog pounds that offer pets for adoption are asked to cooperate with our program by giving puppies and kittens only to those who pay in advance for the spaying or altering of the animal. We administer this policy through our certificate system.

Corps of Volunteers. The educational program is under way throughout the United States. Our subsidy program is active in many communities. As our funds and corps of volunteers grow we shall extend our efforts to other areas, so that all Americans can help prevent the unplanned birth of these dependent animals.

HOW YOU CAN BE A FRIEND OF ANIMALS

(1) Have your pet spayed unless you personally plan to keep and care for the litters. (2) Help us carry on this work by contributing to Friends of Animals, Inc. (3) Remember that each animal spayed prevents the yearly production of at least two litters of unwanted puppies or kittens. (4) Join Friends of Animals.

Try to locate an advertising layout artist to help you make this attractive, since the general impression made by the brochure itself will give an impression about your club which may be as important as the things you say in the copy.

OTHER PRINTED MATERIAL

The picture of your organization created by your brochure or fact sheet can be brought into sharper focus by appropriate letterheads, envelopes, business cards, and other printed materials which give instant identification and recognition. These permanent media reinforce the transitory news stories and announcements and help establish its public image.

If you send your release typed on printed letterhead or on a printed release form, the immediate impression will be more favorable, and this will help build respect for your group among editors and newscasters. And of course letters on club stationery enhance the image of any organization.

In getting stationery printed it is well to anticipate the possibility of address changes. If you use the address of one of the officers, when new officers are elected the stationery is out of date. An address which is crossed out and changed in ink no longer looks professional. To avoid this, try to use an address that will be permanent. And do not get a larger quantity of stationery than you will use up in a reasonable time.

If the names of club officers are printed on stationery the problem is even more acute. Don't let the printer talk you into ordering more than will be used during their term of office, even though the additional hundreds cost much less than the first hundred.

The quality of paper on which your letterhead is printed has a subtle effect in making an impression on the person who reads your letters. Ask the printer to use a good quality rag bond paper.

If you don't have a special printed form on which to type your news releases, you might consider the possibility of having a supply of letterhead run on a cheaper quality paper for this purpose. If your club can afford a printed form for your news releases, this is impressive. Two sample news releases follow.

TV COMEDY WRITER TO ADDRESS WRITING CLASS

Jack Hanrahan of the comedy team that writes for the Rowan & Martin "Laugh-In" will speak to the Writing for Publication class at West Valley Occupational Center 9:30 a.m. Monday, May 12, according to Morgan Harris, instructor.

Hanrahan and his teammate Phil Hahn are head writers for "Laugh-In." They won an Emmy for comedy variety and have written for such shows as Get Smart, Jackie Gleason, Mike Douglas, Merv Griffin, and Westinghouse. In addition to his TV writing, Hanrahan has written humor books for children and political satire for their parents and has contributed to *Mad, Playboy,* the *Saturday Evening Post,* and other publications.

He will talk to the writing class about problems he has met as a writer of humor and how he dealt with them. He will then answer questions from the class. This session of the class is open to the public. It meets from 9:30 a.m. to 12:30 p.m. in Room 1 at the Center, 6200 Winnetka Avenue, Woodland Hills. Dr. Calvin Dellefield, center director, said there is ample parking on the north end of the campus and visitors are welcome.

West Valley Occupational Center's course in Writing for Publication prepares trainees to enter the field of professional writing, with emphasis on techniques and trade practices of freelance writing.

WRITERS' WORKSHOP TO HEAR
LOCAL AUTHOR

Verne T. Davis, author, will speak for the Writers' Workshop of the Adult Occupational Training Center. Friday morning, November 19. A former contractor in the field of heavy construction, Davis turned to writing for juveniles upon his retirement. His first book, *The Time of the Wolves*, was published after he was 70 years of age. It was an immediate success, recommended by both the *Librarians Journal* and *Publisher's Weekly*.

Two other books followed: *The Gobbler Called* and *The Runaway Cattle*. His publisher, Morrow, has scheduled for publication next April his fourth book, *The Devil Cat Screamed*.

Davis has studied with Morgan Harris, director of the Writers' Workshop, and he will share with workshop members and guests anecdotes from his experience in writing for young people.

This meeting is open to the public, according to Harris, who emphasizes that anyone interested in writing will be welcome to this or any other session of the workshop which meets from 9:30 to 12:30 Friday mornings in Room 2 of the Adult Occupational Training Center, 6200 Winnetka Avenue, Woodland Hills.

The use of colored ink in printing stationery is an expensive affectation which is only justified if the most extreme efforts are being made to establish the status of the organization. Sometimes blue or brown typewriter ribbons are used, and the printer uses an ink which matches when he prints the stationery. Such refinements are costly, and for most organizations they are not worth the money and meticulous care they require. Black printing on white paper is always in good taste.

On the other hand, the monthly newsletter or club bulletin which survives with the handicap of being mimeographed may appropriately use a colored masthead to give it a professional appearance and help it to get the attention it deserves.

You will find a supply of business cards useful in your work as publicity chairman. In most situations the least expensive cards are just as effective as those costing more. Try to avoid getting too many. Most printers do not want to set up the type for a run of less than a thousand, whereas you may never use more than a few hundred and the balance becomes wastepaper.

THE COST OF PRINTING

To save money on printing your brochure, letterheads, and all other printing, get bids from several printers. Be sure each one is bidding on the same thing. This means you must specify not only quantity, but also kind and quality of paper.

You can ask the first printer from whom you get a bid to specify in detail what he is bidding on. Then you can use these specifications in asking for bids.

PUBLIC IMAGE

The public image of your club is made up of the sum total of all the impressions that people have of your club. This means both the impressions they get from the printed material you produce—the news stories, announcements, advertisements, and posters you send out—and also the impression they get from the behavior of club members. The way you and the other officers and members greet a reporter or the receptionist at the radio station or the printer are impressions which are added up to become the public image of your club.

You can't control all of this, of course, but people do tend to see what they expect to see, and you can help to focus their expectations on the image you have selected.

Chapter 10

How To Publicize Special Events

WHAT'S A SPECIAL EVENT?

Each year since 1865 the Jumping Frog Jubilee in Angels Camp, California, has gotten a lot of favorable publicity and brought many visitors to the town. Frog-jumping enthusiasts compete for fun and for the $1200 prize in the Grand Final Competition. The entry fees, frog rental fees, jockey rental fees, and Frogtown Airport service fees defray the expenses and raise money for civic purposes.

This is a special event. So is a circus, an exhibit of classic cars, a dance, an arts and crafts fair, a banquet, a display of war figures, a flower show, a convention, an auto race, a fashion luncheon, a parade, an art show—the list is endless.

The monthly meeting of your club is not a special event. "Special" means something different, something that is not frequent and regular, although some regular events are special in the lives of the participants and are handled as special events.

"Event" in this usage, means anything that brings people together because of a shared interest. Of course a major catastrophe, such as the crash of an airliner, does not happen regularly (thank God!), and it may cause people to gather because of a shared interest—more specifically a shared curiosity. But we are talking about planned special events in which people are brought together for a purpose.

The purpose of those who attend may be to be entertained or to be fed or to learn something more about classic cars or flower arrangements. The purpose of the sponsoring organization may be to call attention to its services, to enlist public support, to gain members, to honor someone, or to promote some idea. Most often it is to raise funds.

THE PURPOSE COMES FIRST

Chapter 2 pointed out that the first step to success in any undertaking is to define the goal. In deciding to stage a special event and in choosing the kind of an event to present, you need to be clear about what you are trying to do. What is your purpose?

Only when you have your purpose clearly in mind can you answer the question "Is the special event the best way to achieve this?" If the answer is "yes," the next question is "What kind of a special event—that we can put on—will do it best?"

There are all kinds of events, more than you could list. Some, such as conventions, trade shows, or store openings, require the work of hundreds and even thousands of people; others, such as luncheons and fashion shows and picnics, can be presented by a small group.

A popular type of special event is an anniversary. The one you celebrate need not even be an anniversary of your own organization. Your club can initiate and coordinate a celebration of the founding of your town or some historical event of importance. Other people and groups will participate and help out, but your organization will reap the chief benefit because it is in charge. The news releases will mention your organization as the coordinating body. Others will turn to you for information, ideas, and direction.

Anniversaries which commemorate events make colorful presentations because they encourage the wearing of old-fashioned costumes, bringing antiques out from the attics and garages in town, and eliciting reminiscences and stories from old-timers.

You can also celebrate current events with ceremonies to formally open a new bridge or highway or public library. Or you can feature the official opening of your new club or lodge building.

Balls and banquets can be enjoyed by as many people as you can take care of. You can have carnivals or concerts or conferences. Special events need not be big and complex; they can be simple like an ice-cream social or an opening night.

A contest makes a fine special event, with awards given on a TV program or at an awards banquet. These can be art contests, beauty contests, baby contests, or contests for the best posters or slogans or letters. You can often get the prizes donated by business firms in town in return for the publicity they will get as donors.

AN EVENT WITHIN AN EVENT

You can sometimes have an event within an event, such as a garden exhibit by a women's club at a county fair. The promoters of the fair are usually glad to coordinate activities this way. By distributing publicity among your members and others for your garden exhibit, you help swell the crowds at the fair. At the same time, by being there, your garden exhibit is seen by the crowds who come to the fair for other interests.

Whenever others are presenting something that will attract crowds, you can talk with them about cooperating for mutual advantage. If there is to be a trade fair such as an auto show, you might arrange to have a "Boy Scout Day" if you are publicity chairman for the Boy Scouts or a "Local Artists Day" if yours is an art club.

One type of money-raising event that is very popular is an auction of items contributed by celebrities and other VIPs. Those who give items to be auctioned do not need to be auctioned for a good cause.

Related to this, in major cities there are auctioneers who will put on a benefit art auction for any organization that can turn out a crowd. These can be used both to raise money and to solicit memberships.

A Sunday afternoon benefit garden party at which the people who attend—at a fee—can meet celebrities is a money-making gimmick you can use if you have VIPs who will lend their presence for the cause. If they are authors or artists you can have their books or pictures there for sale, which will add to the income.

APPRECIATION

Some special events are for the "in group," such as the employees of a business or the members of a club or church or synagogue. These can be picnics, shows, auctions, parties, dances, contests, or luncheons. The highlight of such an event might be the giving of awards to individuals for distinguished service to the organization. There is nothing like appreciation to make people feel great and to encourage further participation in activities—both by those who receive awards and by those who would like to receive similar recognition another year.

When you give public recognition for service, be sure no deserving person is omitted. When in doubt, include them. You don't have to give expensive items; merely reading their names aloud as "honorable mention" is often enough. An inexpensive printed certificate of appreciation is usually worth many times its cost.

In choosing special events, keep in mind that the armed forces of the United States spend a lot of money on public relations. As a result you can get all kinds of help: a military band, a drill corps, tanks, flags, and glamour. Ask their local public relations office for ideas. For example, maybe the Navy will let you bring guests aboard a submarine to see how it looks inside.

Many different things can be special events: a parade, a karate exhibition, a pancake breakfast, a European tour, a swap meet, a pet show, an Easter sunrise service, a cooking school, a barbecue, or a regatta.

Nobody owns ideas. Anything that anyone else has done, you may be able to do better. So go ahead and adopt and adapt any ideas that you have seen others use with success.

PLANNING

Having chosen the special event, the sponsoring organization should appoint someone to coordinate all activities in connection with it. He can work with a steering committee, and you should be one of the members. This committee should plan every step.

The functions of the steering committee can be subdivided into dealing with people, programs, and promotion.

People

One section of the steering committee will be responsible for community contacts. They may start with the mayor or the governor, arranging to get proclamations made and inviting one of these dignitaries or some other popular public official to open the festivities. They may work with members of the city council to get resolutions passed. If the event will have any effect on traffic, they may consult with the chief of police.

They can contact leaders in other organizations to get cooperation and to forestall criticism or opposition in some cases. They may solicit contributions of cash or services or personnel from various businesses and get whatever help is possible from schools, churches, social and civic clubs, and other groups.

Programs

The program is the event itself. The section of the steering committee handling program arrangements should be responsible for every detail in presenting something that people will come to see or hear or do. They can set the date, arrange for the auditorium or banquet facilities or location, decide which speaker or circus to get, choose a caterer, and work out a budget. They should schedule the tasks to be completed prior to the big day and approve the agenda for the event itself.

Some members of this section can be in charge of ticket sales and others in charge of the how itself—or the banquet or the exhibit. Some can be responsible for personnel at the event.

Promotion

All the preceding is someone else's responsibility—not yours. Your responsibility is promotion—planning the publicity and advertising—and seeing that your plans are carried out. It is a big enough task in itself.

You are on the committee because you need to be there when the plans are being made for two purposes: (1) to check on suggestions from the standpoint of publicity and help the committee arrive at plans that will appeal to the greatest number of people, and (2) when you get back to your desk to plan and prepare the publicity you will know what is being done and how to present it.

PLANNING THE PUBLICITY

For the best possible campaign that will sell all the tickets, fill the auditorium, and leave standing room only you need ample time, ample money, and ample personnel. You are not likely to have all three.

Time

It is always later than you think. To get ample time you must have the date set farther ahead than anyone believes necessary.

Money

You are not likely to have ample money but, in any case, budget what you have. This means that before you begin to do any planning or dreaming up of publicity ideas you should find out what you can spend.

There is one exception to this. If you are in the fortunate situation of being able to ask for the amount you will need, then you must do some planning and develop an estimate of costs before you make your request so you will know what amount to ask for. But if the amount you can spend for publicity is fixed regardless of your plans and ideas, then find out what the amount is before you begin to plan.

In your plan, provide for every cost. If it can't be paid for, you can't do it no matter how effective it would be as a publicity effort. Forget it.

If you can locate financial records of previous events, you will find them of immense help in making out your budget. If you can't get them from your own organization, perhaps you can find the records of a special event staged by some other group. It is a great saving of time and of mistakes if you can pattern after what someone has already done. This is true not only in budgeting but in every operation.

The plan, with its estimate of costs for each item, constitutes your budget. Make it total 15% less than the amount you have to spend. The balance is a cushion for (1) things you didn't anticipate, (2) changes in costs, (3) new opportunities that turn up during the campaign which are too important to miss, and (4) your own peace of mind in knowing that you have a small reserve available for emergencies.

Personnel

Let us hope you took seriously the comments in Chapter 2 on developing a file of resource people among your membership so that now you will find it relatively easy to create a publicity committee to work with you on the campaign for the special event.

Start with internal publicity. Your first task is to inform the members of your own organization of the forthcoming event and the initial steps being taken to build up to it. Their enthusiasm is basic to the success of almost every special event. They will be called on to participate in many ways: serving on committees in preparation for the event; making costumes, decorations, and refreshments; distributing handbills; putting up posters telling their friends; selling tickets; serving as hostesses, ushers, and parking lot attendants; bringing their families and guests; and cleaning up afterward.

All the members of the steering committee should be aware of the importance of selling the program to the membership first and developing enthusiasm. The members, in turn, should help sell it to outsiders and bring the crowd.

MAKE A SEPARATE PLAN

Internal publicity for the special event can be carried in the newsletter, featured in notices on the bulletin board, told about at meetings, broadcast via the telephone tree, distributed through mailings to individuals, and—most important—spread by word of mouth starting with each member of the steering committee and each member of your publicity committee.

Don't let the matter of internal publicity expire in good intentions. Make a separate plan and a schedule of steps to be taken to reach your own members—the "in group."

One of the satisfying things about handling publicity is the opportunity you have to reward these people by mentioning them in connection with the volunteer tasks they are doing. Such recognition of the value of their contribution is of tremendous importance to them—and therefore of equal importance to you and to the organization.

It costs you nothing, so be lavish with recognition and appreciation. Mention them in stories for the newspaper and again in the newsletter, and give them credits in the printed program of the event. *Important:* Get one of your helpers to doublecheck to be sure no one has been overlooked or omitted.

External publicity is for nonmembers. With one important exception, you are interested only in a limited group—those that are prospects and might attend the special event you are promoting. Economy and effectiveness in publicity, as in advertising, begins with making an accurate selection of prospects and getting your message to them and not wasting money and effort pushing your message onto people who are not going to respond no matter what you do.

PICK YOUR PROSPECTS

To raise money the Women's Club of Imaginary City decided to present a speaker in the community auditorium. They engaged a well-known author who was extremely popular with the younger generation. He had packed the auditorium of a nearby college shortly before, and had people standing in the halls outside to hear him.

The Women's Club gave 10 tickets each to all members, asking them to sell the tickets at $1 each. They publicized the lecture in the club newsletter. Since the lecturer had a big name, they expected 1000 people. They had only 300. Most of the members paid for a ticket for themselves and their husbands and returned the rest, reporting, "I couldn't sell them."

The failure was due entirely to an inadequate evaluation of the prospects. The friends of the club members were not admirers and supporters of the author. The younger people, among whom he had hundreds of followers, were not the ones asked to purchase tickets.

This event might have been a great success had the advertising and announcements been pitched to the younger crowd over the radio stations which played their kind of music, through college newspapers, and through broad general newspaper coverage.

Moral: Be selective. Discuss with the steering committee who the prospects are, and get all the help you can in delineating your audience so that your announcements get to the right people—those who are interested in what you are offering them.

SHARPSHOOTING WITH MAILING LISTS

Direct mail is a means of sharpshooting so that your material goes to exactly the people you want it to go to. Through the right mailing lists you can reach the right people.

With the passage of time, mailing lists become increasingly inaccurate. Your first mailing in any campaign should not only carry a message but should also cleanup the list. You have probably noticed on envelopes the phrase "address correction requested." These mailers have made arrangements with the post office to have forwarding addresses supplied to them for people who have moved. By doing this you can correct your own mailing list.

There are firms which specialize in maintaining mailing lists belonging to their clients. If your mailing operations are substantial you can use their services. They are listed in the yellow pages of the phone book under "Mailing Lists."

If your mailing list is small and you want to handle it in your own office, you should know about mailing stickers—8½ × 11 inch gummed sheets perforated into 33 stickers. These come padded in groups of three or four sheets with carbons already inserted. You can type addresses and make copies of them at the same time. Since these may smudge a bit in storage, use the last carbon copy for your first mailing, retaining the better copies for later use.

A minor tragedy that you want to avoid is finding yourself in competition with another organization for the same prospects. If one organization is putting on a flower show the same day that another group is staging a fashion show, they may be competing for the same people, and each will interfere with the success of the other.

To avoid getting caught in such a situation, get out a publicity release far enough in advance to forestall any other group making plans for what would be a competing attraction on the same date. To make sure it comes to their attention you can mail them a copy of the release or of the news story when it appears, together with a friendly letter inviting their cooperation. This is part of the responsibility of the community contacts section of the steering committee, so coordinate it with them.

THE PROMOTION CAMPAIGN

Unless it is a very small event, the promotion campaign is a bigger task than you can handle by yourself. Your committee can include as many people as you can get to help you. Its first natural division is into one section to handle publicity and another to handle advertising.

Publicity can be divided into types of outlets, such as newspapers, magazines, TV and radio, public speakers who will appear before service clubs and other groups, and so forth. The use of paid advertising needs to be closely coordinated with the publicity, since those who give publicity space or air time free will naturally and rightfully expect to be those with whom you will spend your advertising funds.

You will need an artist and layout person who can do pasteup; you can use copywriters and letter writers, a photographer, and a number of secretaries, typists, and clerical and office helpers.

YOUR SCHEDULE IS YOUR PLAN

A good campaign gets underway slowly and gains increasing tempo. There may be several weeks between the first news release and the second. But by the end of the campaign, there may be news releases and public service announcements going out daily.

This doesn't mean you move faster and faster. It means preparing things ahead of time so they are ready to be used, like stocking an arsenal of ammunition to be fired when it is needed.

To work out a schedule to fit the increasing tempo, you may plan the beginning of it in months and the latter part in weeks. For instance, let's assume an event will occur June 3. Layout a program to cover five months as follows.

First month/January: Press release (also radio and TV) announcing the event and the date, time, and place. This story describes what the event is to be and what its objectives are. It covers steps leading up to the decision to hold the event and gives full information on the sponsoring group.

Send a copy of this story to other organizations in the community together with a note from the community contacts chairman inviting their cooperation. This serves to preempt the date so they will not schedule a competing event too close to that time.

Second month/February: First week—Perhaps a month after the first announcement, issue a story naming the chairman who is coordinating the event and a brief resume of his position in the business community. Include a quotation from him expressing his enthusiasm and telling why he is willing to undertake this important assignment.

His photograph should accompany this story, together with a quotation by the president of the group commending the coordinating chairman and further boosting the event. Describe its purposes more fully, showing its importance to the community and the readers.

Third week—Announce the creation of the steering committee. and name the major committeemen who will be in charge of community contacts.

Fourth week—Issue release announcing names of committeemen in charge of program arrangements and inviting those who wish to help with certain tasks to contact the people you name in your story.

Third month/March: First week—Story announcing stars or speaker and other participants in the event.

Second week—Background story giving historical data about the anniversary being celebrated or the bridge being opened and dedicated or other human interest material.

Third week—Get out items for the TV and radio "community calendar."

Fourth week—Story giving dates of rehearsals, new developments. additional sponsors, and other contributors.

Fourth month/April: First week—Get out "fact sheet" for all media. and mail copies to other groups in town.

Second week—Background story about sponsoring group, its history. progress. previous events it has presented, position in the community. and role in the event. Cover the officers of the group and the leaders who are contributing their time to this event. Mention their other activities in the community. Explain the philosophy and goals of the group and how this event furthers those goals. Photographs of officers, headquarters. and others may accompany this story.

Third week—News release of progress announced by coordinating committee. Give highlights of reports by individual chairmen. Include appeal for additional anecdotes, historical items. costumes, antiques, or any other items needed. Photo of committee member displaying flag or check or costume.

Fourth week—TV interviews with celebrities who are to appear. or with officrs of the coordinating committee. Make dates for speakers to appear before schools, service clubs, and so on.

Fifth month/May: First week—new developments, new participants. Arrange for a feature story in the Sunday edition of the paper.

Second week—Send out press invitations.

Third week—Get out press kit including all press releases sent out to date. additional stories covering every facet of the event, history of the sponsoring organization, fact sheet about the organization and its purposes and contribution to the community, agenda for the event, guest list, copies of luncheon or dinner menu, copies of speeches and resolutions and proclamations, biographies of important members, and photographs of important members and officers and entertainers.

Fourth week—TV interview with celebrity. Wrapup story, fillers, and public service announcements on TV and radio.

Sixth month, June: The big week—Week of the event: Story recapitulating all significant details of event (what, when, where, who, why—especially why—and sometimes how). Announce last-minute changes or developments, something perhaps that you have known about but have saved for this spot.

POST THE SCHEDULE

When you have completed your master publicity and promotion schedule, post it where everyone involved will see it. Give copies to chairmen of important committees and others who may be helpful in supplying you with information for your stories.

Have several people active in welcoming members of the press and TV and radio representatives. Make your arrangements well in advance. Have a "pressroom" labeled "FOR PRESS ONLY." It can be a hotel room, store, office, or whatever you can arrange. Be sure it is staffed by members of your publicity committee prepared to help the news media in any way possible. Instruct the members who are staffing it to see that no one gets in except newsmen. Kibitzers like to crowd in where they think the newsmen are. Keep them out.

Have a stock of press release material, press kits, last-minute stories, and a brief recap of what is going on. Provide chairs and tables, typewriters and paper, telephones, pads and pencils, and messengers.

Provide a special parking area near the pressroom, and arrange to have volunteers on hand to transport reporters who want to go someplace.

At smaller, indoor events, such as a luncheon or banquet, have a press table as near as possible to the speaker's table and close to an exit so reporters and photographers can come and go without disturbing the meeting. Note the location of the nearest telephone so you can direct a reporter to it if he asks.

FOLLOW-THROUGH

Telephone the editors of newspapers who send representatives and ask each one if he got all the information he needs. If he does want additional information, get it to him fast because he is working against a deadline—and if the material is not there, your story is out.

Get out thank you notes to everybody: to the people in our organization who helped; to people in other organizations who helped or thought they helped; to participants, celebrities, officials, newspaper reporters and editors, TV reporters, radio people, and everyone who had anything to do with the event. Write special notes of appreciation to the members of your own committee.

This may take several days, but for you the special event is not finished until this is done. (After that you can collapse.)

PRESS INVITATIONS

An effective type of press invitation is the "press memo" which usually reads as follows:

PRESS MEMO   City editor
TO: Society editor
                     Photo editor

FROM: Edgar Jackson, publicity chairman

SUBJECT: Garden City Women's Club Fashion Luncheon

DATE: Saturday, June 3

PLACE: Ballroom of Women's Club House
                     613 Cataline Street
                     Belleville, New York

TIME: 12 noon

Then fill in whatever other information is pertinent such as dais guests and speakers and subjects.

Be sure to note at the bottom:

Tables are reserved for the press

CHECKLIST OF ITEMS FOR STORIES

[ ] New developments: names of new volunteers or the total number of participants; announcement of personalities scheduled to participate; finishing touches being put to a bridge, building, exhibits, etc.

[ ] Announcement of guest speakers and topics.

[ ] Photos of VIPs or public officials buying first ticket, workman nailing in last board or laying last brick, child tacking up a sign, chairman welcoming celebrity at airport, mountains, merchandise, exhibits, animals, performers, or clowns.

[ ] Date, time, and location of event.

[ ] Anticipated attendance and nature of event.

[ ] Guest speakers and subjects they will discuss.

[ ] Special entertainment or entertainers.

[ ] Honored guests: names and positions in business or political life.

[ ] Special menus.

[ ] Receptions to precede the event.

[ ] List of outgoing officers and nominees for new positions.

[ ] Closing dinner, dance, speaker.

[ ] Unusual displays and exhibits.

[ ] Giveaways: balloons, refreshments, flowers, toys, etc.

[ ] Profiles of chairmen of event, entertainers, managers, other VIPs.

[ ] Unique items or services: baby-sitting provisions, etc.

[ ] Historical data, background material, costs of display, fireworks, etc.

[ ] Floats, parades, contests, participants.

Chapter 11

Advertising and Promotion Checklist

These items, arranged alphabetically, are worthy of more than a superficial reading. You should review this list periodically. Take one item at a time that does not appear to be immediately applicable to your needs, and turn it over in your mind. Combine it with others in various ways, and modify it slightly. With a little creative thought you may be able to adapt it to your purpose so that what appeared at first to be useless may turn out to be the source of the most effective publicity promotion of your entire year.

ANNOUNCEMENTS. Written or printed pieces giving notice of special events, meetings, etc. Carries the "public image" to those who see it.

BALLOONS. A balloon in the hand of a child makes a joyous statement. Printed advertising on balloons in the hands of 500 children makes a resounding statement for the advertiser. Balloons communicate a festive occasion—New Year's Eve, Mardi Gras, etc. Look up "balloons" in the yellow pages of your telephone directory.

BILLBOARDS. See "outdoor advertising." These super posters are nearly everywhere. They cost money and time—three to four months from inception to public viewing.

BLUEPRINTS. A blueprint is a way to get a poster reproduced that is not often used. Therefore it has the advantage of being different. Besides the usual white on blue, it is possible to obtain a "blue line positive" which is blue on a white background. Color can be added with crayon. The paper comes in 100 yard rolls in different widths at architectural supply houses. It is not expensive. In your inventory of talent and sources among members, don't overlook architects.

BOTTLES. Bottlers of various kinds of drinks can be approached for a cooperative advertising of "tie-in" promotion. Die cut advertising pieces can be printed and placed around the necks of bottles. The tops can be used for a printed message, too.

BOOKLETS. If your organization has an interesting history, a book can be written about it. A professional writer is a must.

BROADCASTS, RADIO AND TELEVISION. Public service time is free. See Chapter 7.

BROADSIDE. Mimeographed or printed, this ubiquitous piece of advertising is a single halfsheet or full sheet of paper, printed on one side, opening to a single sheet, and intended for quick reading.

BROCHURE. Usually more elaborate than a booklet, this is a term used loosely for any promotional pamphlet.

BULLETINS. Churches, luncheon clubs, and similar organizations that must maintain a high level of attendance at regular meetings ordinarily publish a bulletin to remind members about the meetings, tell about events coming up, and give committee reports and other information that would be too much for a postcard to carry.

These can be reproduced by offset printing or multigraph for a cent or less per copy. See Chapter 10.

BULLETIN BOARDS. Who doesn't remember this one from school, church, or work? News or announcements are posted periodically. Train your members to read them.

CALENDARS. Imprinted with the name of a business or organization and its message. Sometimes given out for good will; sometimes sold to raise funds. UNICEF's calendar featuring young artists is an example in fund raising.

CAMPAIGN. An all-out publicity-promotion-advertising effort which uses all possible means of getting the message across.

CAR CARDS. Small posters displayed in trolleys and buses, subways, and elevated trains. If you supply the posters you may be able to promote the space free of charge. Look up "advertising-transit" in the yellow pages of the phone book for information on who leases space.

CARTOONS. If you have an artist in your group, or more specifically a cartoonist, think up an idea for a cartoon and write a gag line. Have it made the size your newspaper can use, and pay for the cost of producing it from your funds.

CATALOGS. A reference book including illustrations, descriptions, and other data.

CIRCULARS. One sheet of printed paper produced for inexpensive, widespread distribution through mailing or hauling out. These can be distributed at meetings: summarizing the points made by the speaker, telling the readers things they can do in a numbered list, and giving facts and arguments for them to use in "selling" the project to their friends and neighbors. You can use them as questionnaires to get information across or to call attention to specific items.

CLASSIFIED ADS. The use of these for unusual purposes can be an effective way of calling attention to your project. For instance:

> Dear Eddie: I'm getting away from it all by going on the Cranston Club's annual weekend outing to Calm Lake July 17—19. Why don't you come with us? Love, Josephine.

CLIPSHEET. A sheet of paper containing news stories and other newspaper items, printed on one side, and sent out regularly by institutions to a list of newspapers and publishers. Editors may clip these stories and print them.

CLUB MOTTO. Club mottos serve as reminders. "Be prepared" brings to mind the picture of a Boy Scout.

COLUMNIST. If you pick up an item that could be used by a columnist for his paper, pass it on to him. Don't limit this to things that have to do with your job as publicity chairman. You are building goodwill. It's like money in the bank.

If he uses half a dozen items you have suppied him during the year, when the day comes that you want a writeup about some event in your club, he will be glad to repay some of his debt to you. No matter how badly he mangles any item you give him, smile. After all, you are getting free publicity; even if it isn't as good as you want, thank him.

COMIC BOOKS. Use of the comic strip method to tell a story is growing in popularity. Some publishers specialize in books with coloring pictures, quizzes, and games for poor readers. Others produce books directed at a well-educated clientele. These books are being used to sell products, win votes, raise money, organize workers, educate, and put over other messages. People in lower educational levels and poor readers respond to comics-type material. They are especially valuable when communicating with children.

COMPANY PUBLICATIONS. House organs, bulletins, etc.. limited to certain subjects and designed to appeal to well-defined groups.

CONTESTS. A contest is a news event, usually good for a story in the paper. You can stage beauty contests, watermelon eating contests, frog jumping contests, poster contests, slogan contests—all kinds of contests. Be sure the judges are fair and that you give an award, even if it is only a certificate or a ribbon.

CONTINUITY STRIP. An advertisement that simulates a comic strip and tells a complete story in plot sequence.

DIRECT MAIL ADVERTISING. Printed matter mailed to prospects. A small mailing to the right selected list of people, inviting them to your fashion show or spring dance might pay off. Success depends on three things: the right mailing piece, the right list of people to send it to, and the right timing of the mailing.

This is a specialty field, and it would be wise to seek the counsel of an advertising person experienced in direct mail before you spend much money for mailings.

DIRECTORIES. You can list your organization's name in a directory. The telephone book is one directory, but check on this before you order the listing. If you are using a residence phone and you ask for a listing as an organization, the phone company may require you to pay a business rate.

Other directories are published by chambers of commerce, churches, and other organizations.

DISPLAYS. Displays in store windows, business firms, and financial institutions such as banks and loan companies will call attention to your activities. Merchants are experts at this. One merchant had goods delivered onto the sidewalk where his employees unpacked them slowly and carried them slowly into his store, thus enabling passersby to see what merchandise they could buy there.

DROP-IN ADS. Advertising messages added to regular ads that are of a different nature. They are especially useful when a group has a slogan. "Support Your Local Police" is one illustration.

DUPLICATE STICKERS. Gummed stickers that come in perforated sheets, usually 33 to the sheet. They are used mostly as address labels. Using carbons, three or four can be typed at a time. They are then torn off and pasted onto the envelope or mailer. They can be purchased as single sheets or in pads with carbon already inserted.

FACSIMILE. An exact copy or reproduction of something, usually produced by a mechanical or photographic process from the original.

Creativeness often consists of merely turning up, or over, what is there already. The Film Welfare League had a stock of photographs of its members in costumes; some black and white, others in color. When a costume party needed publicizing, the publicity chairman sent some of these snapshots to a photographer and had them blown up to poster size. These giant photos were then mounted on poster boards from the art store and lettered with information to attract the public.

FACT SHEET. A fact sheet is basic to every organization. It gives elementary information about the group and states its purpose, its methods, and its achievements. It may include names, addresses, and telephone numbers. These are sometimes sent along with news releases and requests for space and time.

FILLERS. A short bit of copy used to fill out a blank space at the end of a newspaper column or at the end of an article in a magazine. These are useful to the publicity chairman to keep his group in the public eye.

FILMSTRIPS. A continuous strip of film in which the frames are presented in a fixed sequence, but not simulating motion. Sometimes a sound track is synchronized to the frames. More often the operator reads a typed script as the pictures appear on the screen. You can rent a filmstrip projector and screen.

FLANNEL BOARD. A board covered with flannel on which you can stick things and use as a visual aid.

FLAGS. Flags and pennants and banners provide an effective method of conveying a theme and identifying a group or cause. Flags have always symbolized a special event. The more you drape a town with flags and banners, the more festive the occasion becomes.

FLYER. A mailing piece announcing or promoting a special event or special offer.

FOLDER. An 8½ × 11 inch sheet folded twice to create six panels of type and illustration. Sometimes a four-page printed piece. Handy for mailing or giving out. Also a heavy paper container for other papers or for filing.

GOODWILL. The public acceptance of a business or institution. The favorable attitude maintained toward persons, institutions, or groups by others. The continuing object in public relations is to develop and enhance goodwill.

HOME MOVIES. These can be used to good effect both within your group (internal publicity) and with others. You can show movies of play rehearsals, choir practice, or scenes from last year's fashion show or dance to stir enthusiasm among your own members and also to promote bookings before other organizations.

Movies of children at summer camp can be used as part of the pitch to get support for benefits that raise money to send more children to camp this year.

IDENTIFICATION BADGES. Important for officials and gracious for guests. ID badges and "stick-ons" can have your club name in large letters at the top.

IMAGE. The subconscious (or sometimes conscious) impression the public or an individual has of an organization, institution, or person. One goal of publicity is to build a good public image. Good taste in printed matter is important in building the public image. All personal contacts contribute to—or detract from—the public image both of the person and of the organization he represents.

INSERTS. Printed mater enclosed with letters.

INTERNAL PUBLICITY. Messages to your own people: members, staff, employees, the "in group." These are carried by publications, house organs, employee publications, trade journals, bulletin boards, public address announcements, word of mouth, etc.

LAPEL BUTTONS AND ORNAMENTS. The American Legion and Veterans of Foreign Wars have popularized the flag and flower lapel ornament. They use them as fund raisers and get instant recognition which is ultimate publicity.

LEAFLET. A printed piece, usually four pages, that can be used to carry your message.

LETTERHEAD. The name and address printed at the top of a sheet of letter paper is called the letterhead. The same term is used to refer to stationery containing such a heading. In getting stationery printed try to avoid things in your letterhead which will cause it to go out of date, such as the address of a club officer who may be changed. If there is such an item on the letterhead, then order a small enough quantity so that when the officers change there will not be much left to discard.

LETTER. Letters can be sent to members of your own group, other groups, and membership lists you compile or purchase. You can also address "Occupant" or "P. O. Box" and reach specified geographical locations through arrangement with the Post Office. Form letters can be reproduced on automatic typing machines which insert the individual's name in the body of the letter at several points, as well as in the address. This gives a strong personal impact. To find firms that do this kind of work, look in the yellow pages of the phone book under "Letter Shop Service" and within that category find firms that do "Automatic Typing" or "Robotyping" or "Auto-Typing."

Inserts of self-addressed, stamped postcards or envelopes may expedite a response. Instead of using stamped return envelopes, it is possible to obtain a mailing permit from the post office which permits you to print on the envelope that postage will be paid by your organization when the envelope is returned to you.

MAGAZINES. Due to the immense variety of magazines on the American market, it is often possible to place advertisements or articles which will reach selected groups of people and geographical areas. By using special interest magazines, there is a minimum of waste circulation. These are listed in the books *Writer's Market* and *Literary Market Place* at your library.

MAIL ORDER ADVERTISING. This is a type of "Direct Mail Advertising" listed earlier. Its distinguishing feature is that the printed sales pitch mailed to prospects asks them to send an order by return mail. Professionals always test small mailings and compare the results they get from different mailing pieces; then they use the one that produces the greatest response in their mass mailings.

The mail order ads you see repeated again and again are the ones that are paying off. Study them.

MAPS. Buy a map and use it to mark the location of your fair, club picnic, or summer campsite. Reproduce it in an ad, or put it on a bulletin board. Blow it up for background for publicity photographs. With colored pushpins you can outline a zone of activity, locate your membership areas, or delineate a neighborhood covered by solicitors for a charity fund drive. You can devise many uses for maps.

MATCHBOOK ADVERTISING. An interesting means for advertising your club. Your slogan or name can be carried out in colors on matchbook covers and pocketboxes. Matchbook advertising companies offer free design and art services. The Diamond Match Division of Diamond National Corporation offers a variety of sizes, packaging, and promotion plans including distribution ideas.

MENUS. Menu covers or the backs of menus can carry your advertising story. Contact retaurants and motels for space to be donated. You can pay to have menu covers printed with your message and offer them free to eating establishments.

MOCKUP. A scale model used for study, testing, or instruction that can promote interest. If you have plans for a new club house and are raising money for a building site, have a mockup made of the proposed building and display it, perhaps in the window of a financial institution. Mockups get lots of attention because of the scaled down size.

MOTION PICTURES. Some of the first films to come out of Edison's laboratory were produced for advertising purposes. The motion picture business has been around a long time. It can be a key factor in a promotional campaign because of its high impact. Its cost is also high relative to other advertising and publicity.

You can find out about costs from commercial firms whose business is making films for business. They also can tell you about filmstrips, which are much less expensive and may be just as effective for your purposes. If you are going to use a motion picture or a filmstrip as part of your promotional campaign, work with a commercial film-maker.

Before you even consider it, decide on your objectives and know who will be the audience and how you will reach them.

NAPKINS. You can have these specially printed with your message and use them at your next tea, luncheon, or cocktail party. If your budget permits, you can supply them to local restaurants, hotels, refreshment stands, drug and candy stores, malt shops, or barrooms.

NATIONAL "YOU NAME IT" WEEK. Any organization may designate any day, week, or month in recognition of any special event or idea. No formal legal process is required, nor is there any fee or license.

The Apple Tree Press serves as the national clearing house for the recording and announcement of all special events. There is no charge for listing your event.

So if your organization wants to designate July 10—17 as World Federation Week or some other date for something else, write Apple Tree Press in Flint, Michigan and ask for a questionnaire. Fill it out and get it back before August 1 for listing in their calendar the following year.

Follow this up by having your own organization issue a news release, designating the week (day or month) with an official statement. You can strengthen this, of course, by getting the mayor of your city, your county board of supervisors, and the governor of your state to issue a proclamation. On the following page is a proclamation that was submitted to governors for Earth Day. Some proclamations are shorter than this.

NEWSFILM. Newsreel companies film news and sports events for television syndication. Independent stations use this film to supplement their own local news coverage. They prefer one to two minute films, withouh a sound track, plus a script for use by their own announcers.

Because they are news oriented, newsreel companies are particularly suited for producing documentaries with an informational or educational slant. For instance, Hearst Metrotone News in New York produces and distributes sponsored documentary films for showing in school classrooms. Another company is United Press International Newsfilm, also in New York.

NEWSLETTERS. The newsletter is a valuable medium for a publicist because it enjoys an intense, concentrated audience. Newsletters present news and information about a group, project, or specific subject.

NEWSPAPERS. When you buy newspaper space, you are buying readers who are potential prospects for the service or activity or product you are selling. Newspapers are local media and are regarded by their readers as authoritative and legitimate sources of

PROCLAMATION
EARTH DAY 19____

WHEREAS   The citizens of the State of_____together with their fellow human beings in other communities and other lands. have a right to the natural heritage of clean water. fresh air. and clear skies: and

WHEREAS   We have despoiled our environment by releasing deadly radioactive material into the earth. the air. and the water. and by scattering other poisons which contaminate the food we eat and the air we breathe: and

WHEREAS   People depend on other living things. with whom they live in a close symbiotic relationship. We share a common fate with the plankton. the salmon. the pelican. If they are poisoned. we will be poisoned: and

WHEREAS   This planet is our only homeland: if it is destroyed we have no place to go.

NOW THEREFORE let us recognize that our community is a global community. and if it is to serve the needs of any of us. it must serve the needs of all of us: and

LET US harness the enormous powers which. ungoverned. have brought us to this crisis. and use them to recreate the earth and make it again a fruitful and fulling place for all its inhabitants. and

LET US redefine success and progress as things to be measured. not in terms of the gains made by one individual or group or nation at the expense of others. but instead as the improvement of life for the entire community of living things: and

LET US free ourselves from provincial viewpoints. be aware of the earth as a whole. and treat our own backyards as if they were the world and the world as if it were our own backyard: and by these means

LET US make a world we will be happy to have our children grow up in.

LET US begin by observing the day on which most people traditionally celebrate the return of Spring—the vernal equinox—as Earth Day 19___ .

NOW THEREFORE I._____ Governor of the State of_____do hereby proclaim March 21 as "Earth Day 19___." and I urge all citizens. groups. and organizations including governmental bodies to take definite action in relation to that day which will make the earth a better place to live.

IN WITNESS WHEREOF. I have hereunto set my hand and caused the Seal of the State of_____to be affixed this_____day of_____19___.

information: "I read it in the paper." Deadlines for advertising copy are close to the publication deadlines.

NEWS RELEASE. An announcement sent to the media. This is your basic publicity tool. See Chapters 3 and 7.

NEWS SYNDICATES. The publicity worker will find that syndicates of various kinds are good for spreading news over a wide area from any region to the world. Tremendous circulation is obtained with no further trouble and expense than a news story.

Look in the yellow pages of your local phone book under "News Services" or *"Newspaper Feature Syndicates"* or check *Literary Market Place* in your library.

If national publicity is an objective, send a copy of your story to the wire services at the same time you send it to your local papers. Learn the types of syndicates that can help in specific ways. For example, the National Catholic Welfare Conference in Washington, D. C., is an excellent medium for reaching the Catholic readers of America because it directly serves them. Dow-Jones News Service in New York handles business news. They may have an office in a major city near you. Associated Press and United Press International have news bureaus and foreign departments all over the world.

OPEN MIKE RADIO PROGRAMS. Also known as "two-way radio." You can use these local "talk shows" to promote your pet project. Be sure to have all your information at hand, and turn off your own set. See Chapter 8.

OUTDOOR ADVERTISING. Nailing a sign to a tree is advertising out-of-doors. Organized outdoor advertising is an industry which takes four major forms: posters, painted displays, semispectaculars, and spectaculars. Of these four, posters are most frequently used. These are commonly called "billboards." Painted displays are painted walls or painted messages on poster panels.

The semispectacular is a painted bulletin jazzed up with cutout letters, bits that stick out beyond the edge of the bulletin board, special lighting, mechanical parts that move, and three-dimensional effects. The spectacular is constructed of neon lights or incandescent bulbs that are wired and arranged to give the illusion of animation.

Outdoor advertising firms are listed in the phone book. It takes three to four months from the time the poster is designed until it is seen by the public.

PAMPHLETS. Similar to leaflets, containing more pages and having a paper cover.

PARADES. A parade is a wonderful way to get publicity. In England when a bill was before the House of Commons to provide aid for mothers of dependent children, the mothers organized a "perambulator parade" and wheeled baby carriages with signs on them. Such activities not only get the attention of those who view them, they also get into the newspapers and on radio and TV.

Frequently there are parades arranged by a chamber of commerce or some civic organization in which others are invited to participate. Watch for opportunities for your group.

PICKET SIGNS. The recent social revolutions have made these signs well known. There is even one report of a young man carrying a sign reading: "Protest picket for hire, $2 an hour." All you need is a stick, cardboard, and a crayon.

PLACEMATS. For table setups in restaurants or hotel dining rooms, placemats can be used with your message in an attractive layout.

POP. Point of purchase advertising is done at the place where the advertised product is available. Consists of signs, posters, banners, and mobiles in store windows or in the store near where the merchandise is sold. Frequently consists of advertisements—sometimes blown up—that have appeared in natonal magazines or other media.

For example, a series of lectures on marriage were given in a church. The financial secretary set up a card table in the foyer with booklets stacked on it. In the corridor leading into the foyer she hung posters announcing the booklets and the price. Perfect POP.

Salespeople of a national advertiser were instructed to offer to clean the windows of small retail stores, provided the retailer permitted them to place a poster in the window. This offer got retailer consent by offering a free service, but it also was used as a means of removing competitive posters which had been affixed to the windows.

POSTAGE METER IMPRINTS. Envelopes and other items going through the mail can carry a slogan or message in the boxed space ordinarily taken by post office canceling machines. Postage meter companies will tell you about the possibilities and the costs.

POSTERS. May vary from a simple announcement printed with crayon on a piece of cardboard to complicated designs in the manner of miniature state settings. The display should fit the occasion.

Since posters are not read at close range, lettering must be large enough to be legible to people passing by. They may be reproduced in quantity by printing or may be hand lettered by a commercial artist if only a few are needed.

PRESS KITS. A press kit is a sort of looseleaf publicity blueprint prepared by national headquarters to be adapted by local publicity representatives. The cover usually includes a publicity calendar with printed suggestions and space for the local chairman to write in other notes. Often there will be enclosed articles of "canned copy," charts and fillers, photos, and mats for local "planting."

PUBLIC ADDRESS SYSTEMS. In Texas six sound trucks were used to reach 3 million people in an election campaign. A PA system can be mounted on a truck and transported from place to place, presenting speakers and programs as it goes through a widely distributed audience.

Stationary public address systems at any type of mass audience gathering—indoors or outdoors—make it possible to project the human voice to large numbers of people.

PUBLICITY. A message planned, produced, and distributed through selected media to further the particular interest of a client, cause, or group, without payment to media.

PUFF SHEET. A publication that gives favorable publicity to its advertisers.

RADIO. A nonvisual medium. See Chapter 8.

RETURN CARD. A postcard or other card enclosed in a mailing for the convenience of readers who may wish to respond to the message contained in the mailing.

RUBBER STAMPS. A rubber stamp can be created to print a message on envelopes and other items of mail. Sometimes the stamp includes a drawing.

SANDWICH BOARDS. Walking billboards of men or women with two posters hung fore and aft over their shoulders. They make an attention-getting advertisement that costs nothing to put together except time and scrap materials.

SCROLL. The dictionary defines a scroll as a roll of parchment used especially for writing a document. You can hand letter one using Old English or antique lettering on a long sheet of paper with an off-white color that looks like parchment. It makes an out-of-the-ordinary document, whose odd size and appearance will get attention.

Its obvious use is where a scroll would be appropriate—perhaps in announcing a Shakespearean festival, a play or show about English history, or a dance with the theme "When Knighthood Was in Flower." In publicity, however, things are frequently most effective when they are not the obvious.

A scroll can be hung in a suitable place as a sort of elongated poster. To mail copies, roll them up, tie with a suitable colored cord or ribbon, and insert in a mailing tube.

SELF-MAILER. Printed folder prepared to be mailed without a protective cover or envelope. The address is printed or typed on the folder itself, or on a sticker which is pasted onto the self-mailer.

SERVICE COLUMN. A feature column offered without charge to selected newspapers. There are readers for every type of column: sports, gossip, shopping, political, and others. This is a fine publicity tool, but it must not appear to be publicity for a particular institution or individual. It must be of service to the readers.

For instance, if you are handling publicity for an ecology club, you might write a weekly column on ecology supplying readers with information on developments in the field of conservation, recycling, pollution, new laws, or new inventions.

Your column should be short—350 to 500 words. Write half a dozen columns and send them to the editor with an explanatory letter asking if he wants to use this free weekly feature. Enclose a self-addressed, stamped envelope for his reply.

SKYWRITING. Skywriting is one of the most spectacular forms of advertising. It can draw attention to a name or brief message.

SLIDES. These are indvidual pictures, usually shown in groups, with a running commentary spoken or read aloud by the operator. Often advertised as an "illustrated lecture." Slides are much less expensive than a motion picture. While they may not have as potent an impact, it is amazing how intently they hold the attention of an audience.

SLOGANS AND CATCHWORDS. "The quality is remembered long after the price is forgotten." This slogan has probably helped many a do-it-yourself handyman buy a quality tool instead of a cheap one that would have been unsatisfactory. "Peace is a by-product" has encouraged people to be more realistic and less naively emotional in their thinking about peace and war. "Take it easy" has perhaps contributed to longevity in a tense society.

Slogans can be used on bumper stickers, printed in quotes at the bottom of stationery, written as graffiti on walls, printed on cards and stickers, or displayed in ads. They serve as reminders. If you can develop a catchy slogan, it will help fix your idea, club, or activity in the minds of those who see it.

STICKERS. You can have these printed in perforated, gummed sheets and sell them to members to use on their correspondence and elsewhere. Christmas stickers are the outstanding example.

STUNTS. Action gets attention. For example, three runners in track suits with numbers on their backs crouched on the curb at Broadway and Seventh Street. When the light flashed green, they were off, sprinting across Broadway.

Arriving at the other side of the street, they straightened up, walked slowly to the curb of Seventh Street, and crouched there, waiting to sprint across. Back across Broadway, back across Seventh Street, hour after hour. The stunt got attention, raising questions in the minds of the passersby. The answer, passed from person to person, was "they are publicizing the track meet Saturday at the Coliseum."

SYMBOLS. An object or picture may carry instant meaning: a red heart for Valentine's day, Smokey the Bear for fire prevention, Uncle Sam for the United States, and a red cross for the American National Red Cross, or a flag for the nation it represents.

TABLE TENTS. Place cardboard folders that form tents printed with a message on tables at luncheons and in restaurants.

TELEGRAMS. A telegram, though expensive, will command precise, immedite attention that can be aroused by no other means. A simulated telegram can be mailed as printed matter. You can get blank forms from a Western Union office.

TELEPHONE TREE. An effective device for getting a good turnout at meetings and other events. Suppose you have 100 members. Your telephone tree consists of ten "captains" or "district leaders," each of whom has a list of 10 members to phone. When you want to get a message out, you give it to the chairwoman of this group, who gets it into the hands of the captains or district leaders, and each telephones the 10 people on her list. You can reach people in a hurry this way and get a better response, usually, than by a written or printed message.

Frequently the phone call is used as a followup reminder which has already been announced in a mailing.

TELEVISION. A visual medium. See Chapter 8.

TIE-IN. A promotional technique of combining the activities of two or more organizations on one project. Frequently a local firm will run an ad in a newspaper which ties in with a national ad in the same paper.

VISUAL AIDS. Charts, graphs, magnetic boards, blackboards, paper pads, lettered cards, pictures, etc.

Visual aids discipline the audience to center attention on the subject. The material must be presented in a form large enough to be seen by the entire audience. It should illustrate the points being made by the speaker and should not be so complicated that the attention of the audience is distracted trying to figure out what it is.

WORD OF MOUTH. Feelings about things are most quickly expressed by word of mouth. This is perhaps the most subtle of publicity tools. It is not subject to cut-and-dry techniques, like so many publicity tools. Word of mouth spreads with extreme speed and spontaneity if the subject is close to the emotions of people. Ask your members to "talk it up."

Chapter 12

Your Budget

Pity the novice publicity chairman who paid $24.80 out of her own pocket for materials she needed. When she presented the bills to the club treasurer she was told, "There is nothing in the budget for this. I have no funds out of which I can reimburse you."

Cruel? Yes. She feels the club does not appreciate all the time and effort she has put in to plan and produce the publicity. "The least they could do is to pay the necessary expenses and not expect me to pay them."

DON'T SPEND A DIME

This seems only fair, but the president and treasurer have a point: "She made unauthorized expenditures and now expects us to pay for them." Let us hope that her generosity was appreciated by the club, which took a special collection at the next meeting to defray the $24.80. Let us also hope that she learned her lesson: Don't spend a dime until you have made arrangements with the club president and the treasurer as to how you are to be reimbursed.

Normally this will mean that a part of the club budget will be allocated for publicity and promotion. In addition to such a general appropriation, there may be special funds set aside for specific events. If you are putting on an annual fashion show, the expenses of this may be paid from a separate budget for that particular project.

HOW MUCH FOR PUBLICITY?

When the officers come to making up the club budget for the year, they will need to decide how much money the club is going to spend for publicity and promotion. They will want from you a proposed budget, showing what you are going to need and how much it will cost. But what you are going to need depends on what they want to accomplish.

Before a budget can be made up, the executive board should look back and evaluate what was done the previous year. Based on this, they should look ahead and determine the goals for the coming year. When they have done this you can plan a publicity and promotion program as outlined in Chapter 2. The cost of each item in the plan can be calculated or estimated, and these costs constitute the budget.

FORMER RECORDS HELP

Your budgeting will be greatly facilitated if you can work from the records of the preceding year. If such records are not available, try to get a look at the budgets of some organizations similar to yours.

One of the purposes of a budget is to enable you to live within your income. Therefore, a good place to begin is with an estimate of what the income will be for the forthcoming year. If anticipated income is greater than last year, you can increase your expenditures proportionately over last year's budget figures.

BUDGET CHECKLIST

Advertising
  Agency fees
  Newspaper advertising
  Billboards
  Advertising specialties (giveaways, etc.)

Artwork and graphics
  Art supplies
  Photographs
  Posters
  Layouts

Publications
Monthly newsletter
Postage for newsletter
Addressing and mailing newsletter
News releases
Reproduction costs of news releases
Addressing and mailing news releases

Printing
Folders. bulletins. brochures. booklets
Stationery. business cards. etc.
Programs

Office expense
Stationery and office supplies
Repair service on office machines
Duplicating
Telephone and telegraph
Office postage and mailing costs
Messenger and delivery service

Signs and displays
Billboards. artwork. and printing
Display booths for exhibits

Travel and entertainment
Busfare for volunteers
Automobile expense
Dinners for news reporters
Christmas remembrances for people who helped

Contingency fund
Contributions
Emergencies
Special opportunities that cannot be anticipated
Cooperative promotion efforts with other organizations

Miscellaneous
Items which do not fit under another heading
Special events

ITEMS TO INCLUDE

If you are working from a former budget, you don't have to worry much about categories. Most of them will appear in the former budget. You may want to give just a quick glance at the checklist of budget items above to see if it contains any items not in the old budget that you want to include this year.

If you are creating an entirely new budget, without a former one to work from, you may find the checklist helpful, but it is not intended to be an adequate list for any organizatin. The categories listed are only suggestions to aid your thinking in making up a budget that is practical for your needs.

Those items might be arranged and grouped in various ways. For instance, under "Publications" is an item "Addressing and mailing newsletter" and another item "Addressing and mailing news releases." Then under the heading "Office expense" is an item "Office postage and mailing costs." In your budget it might be more practical to put in a single listing to cover all addressing and mailing. You may want to include postage with this or you may want to list it separately.

This will depend on how much you do of what. If you put out only a couple of news releases each month, probably you will not want a separate item in the budget for the cost of addressing and mailing them. But if you send out a great quantity of news releases you may want to list this as a major division of your budget and may even want to include your photographic expense as part of the cost of news releases.

ADVERTISING SPECIALTIES

In planning your program look over the items in Chapter 11 to see if you want to use any of them. If so, get them into the budget.

Here is a sample budget of a community organization working with young people:

XXY Club

PUBLIC RELATIONS

Monthly publication/$500 per month $6,000
   Postage costs of monthly publication.................. 6,000
Printing:
   Brochures, posters, flyers........................... 2,000

Printed material purchased from national office........	1,500
Photos, films, etc..	1,100
Displays and exhibits....................................	300
Community relations (dinner for parents)................	500
	17,400

FUND RAISING

Special Event (Arts & Crafts Fair)......................	300
Special Fund envelopes for contributions................	300
Special Fund booklets....................................	500
Ads, flyers, posters for fund raising campaign...........	200
	1,300
Total budget for year	18,700

Note: This public relations program is carried on from the offices of the club. Office supplies, rent, telephone, mimeographing, secretarial help, postage, and other costs of correspondence are paid for by the club, so they do not appear in this budget.

Here is a record of the expenses for one month of a small organization:

Expenses—June

Envelopes	$9.70
Copies of the Times......................................	.90
Postage..	8.40
Telephone (pro-rate)....................................	1.40
Supplies for poster......................................	2.5
Printer (bill attached)..................................	9.99
Total	32.74

Organizations differ greatly, and it is unlikely that you will find someone else's budget that you can just copy. It won't fit your situation. You will have to work out the categories for a budget that is tailored to the activities and program of your club.

YOU CAN'T HAVE EVERYTHING

Having made your plans and listed all the items you think you are going to need to carry them out, and the cost of each, add it up. It will probably come to quite a bit more than you can hope for.

Now the hard work begins, figuring out what you can cut—what figures you can reduce. What can you get along without? What can you get along with less of?

Expenditures fall into two classes: essential and optional. Optional expenses are desirable, but they can be dispensed with. Buying lunch for a visiting celebrity while waiting for his plane to take off is an optional expense. It is good public relations, but it is not essential. Photographs are often optional, since many newspapers can schedule you a photographer if you follw the steps described in Chapter 6.

In slashing your budget, get it down not just to the point where it is equal to your anticipated income but to a point 10 to 15% less than the income. This much should be listed in your "Contingency fund." Probably it is smarter to divide it between the "Contingency fund" and the "Miscellaneous" heading. That way it is less likely to be questioned—or cut—by the executive board when you present the budget for approval.

The "Contingency fund" is for things you can't anticipate—changes in prices, opportunities that may suddenly come up during the year which should be taken advantage of, or other irregular developments that have not been budgeted for. The "Miscellaneous" category is for items which are too small to merit a separate listing and do not fit into the other catagories. With 10 to 15% of your funds under these two headings, you will be in a strong position to handle emergencies and to take care of purchases that run higher than budget estimates.

APPROVAL OF YOUR BUDGET

In presenting your budget to the executive board for approval, discuss the goals first. Then show how your proposed program will achieve them. If the board has already decided on those goals, and if it likes the program you propose, then the members are prepared to look at your budget figures.

Their first question is likely to be "Are these expenses necessary to carry out these plans?" They may ask you about specific figures in your budget, and you will need to be prepared to tell them how you arrived at each figure—why that item will cost that amount.

If the board members are competent, they will want to know not only that your figues are low enough—that the budget isn't padded or inflated—they will also want to know that your figures are high enough. They want to be assured that if you undertake a project you are not going to have to come to them later and say, "I made a mistake. I can't do this for the amount I asked for. I have to have more money."

There is a tendency on the part of those who have not been through it before to underestimate costs. Be sure you have allowed enough for each item. Glance again at Chapter 9 about the printed items you will need and their cost.

When the board members are satisfied that your estimates are about right, they will want to know "If we appropriate this money, where will it come from?" Your proposed program contains the answer: Its overall effect is to generate income through memberships, subscriptions, sales, contributions, or whatever sources of support your club normally depends on. In addition, the program probably will include one or more special fund-raising events that the board has already decided upon.

If yours is just a tiny budget, you may need only the approval of the president and the treasurer. In this case "two heads are better than one." These officers may be able to offer suggestions for making it a better financial program.

At the same time you ask for approval of the budget, get authorization to spend the money allocated. Work out arrangements for the money you are going to spend—how the bills are to be paid. Are you to have a petty cash fund to be replenished on the basis of receipts you turn in? You will be happier if you get these details settled in advance.

GET RECEIPTS

Keep a record of your expenditures. Get receipts to turn over to the treasurer.

Make a monthly or quarterly summary of expenses and compare this with the financial plan. You will find that some expenses are running more than the budgeted figure and some less. From time to time you may want to revise the budget allocations for the balance of the year to take these changes into consideration.

Bibliography

This guidebook is a manual of practical instruction for the beginner as well as a reference handbook for the experienced publicity chairman.

To make it comprehensive without being bulky, each subject is covered in single chapter. If you want more detailed information, you will find in this list books given over entirely to a single subject, such as style in writing or fund-raising projects. Included also are general books on publicity which are not so comprehensive, but in which you will find some of these ideas in other words—and this is often helpful to the beginner.

Capone, Margaret. *So You've Joined a Club.* Pageant Press, New York, 1954. A helpful book for a newcomer in club work, including a chapter on how to get publicity.

Clay, Roberta. *Promotion in Print: A Guide for Publicity Chairmen.* A. S. Barnes, New York, 1970. Elementary material for the publicity chairman and nonprofessional news writer.

Curtis, Alice P. *Is Your Publicity Showing? A Handbook for the Nonprofessional Chairman.* Van Nostrand Reinhold, New York, 1948. A lightweight, scintillating book of 32 chapters, most of them only two pages with a cheerful cartoon at the beginning.

Cutlip, Scott, and Center, Allen, *Effective Public Relations*. Pentice-Hall, Englewood Cliffs, New Jersey, 1964. A textbook on public relations as a career, written by a vice-president of public relations and a professor of journalism.

Dartnell Press, *The Dartnell Public Relations Handbook*. Dartwell Press, Chicago, 1967. A standard reference book on public relations for professional publicists.

Gluck, Felix, *Modern Publicity*, Viking Press, New York, 1970. Annual compilation of "the best in printed publicity." Color photographs of posters, letterheads, advertisements, and brochures.

Golden, Hal, and Hanson, Kitty, *How to Plan, Produce, and Publicize Special Events*. Oceana Publications, New York, 1960. The authoritative book on this subject, clear, complete, and invaluable.

Golden, Hal, and Hanson, Kitty, *The Technique of Working with the Working Press*. Oceana Publications, New York, 1962. An excellent book showing how to cooperate with—and get cooperation from—the newspapers. Of special value if you are dealing with big city papers.

Gunning, Robert, *The Technique of Clear Writing*, McGraw-Hill, New York, 1952. This book tells you how to make your writing readable so people will understand what you are trying to say.

Hall, Babete, *The Right Angles: How To Do Successful Publicity*. Washburn Ives, New York, 1965. An excellent short handbook which does for the professional, in part, what this guidebook does for the amateur publicity chairman.

Hopkins, Claude, *Scientific Advertising*. Crown Publishers, New York 1960. Basic principles of writing effective advertising copy. The copywriter's "bible."

Jacobs, Herbert, *Practical Publicity, A Handbook for Public and Private Workers*. McGraw-Hill, New York, 1964. Twelve helpful chapters packed with practical information for professionals and nonprofessionals.

Kadon, Ann and John, *Successful Public Relations Techniques*, Modern Schools, Inc., Scottsdale, Arizona, 1976. An elementary textbook written for the home study program of Modern Schools. Chapters on Arranging Press Conferences, Layout, Posters, Direct Mail, Displays and Exhibits. Questions and exercises at end of chapters.

Klein, Ted, and Fred Danzig, *How To Be Heard; Making the Media Work For You.* Macmillan Co., N.Y., 1974. Annotated Table of Contents. Practical, lucid, authoritative manual for consumer activists. Preparing campaigns, organizing supporters, handbills, picketing, legal problems.

Lesly, Philip, Editor, *Public Relations Handbook.* Prentice-Hall, New York, 1967. Leading authorities contribute to this weighty symposium.

Maurello, Ralph, *How To Do Paste-Up and Mechanicals.* Tudor Publishing, New York, 1960. A beautiful, complete book with more illustrations than printing on each page. Every commercial artist should own this book.

McCormick, Mona, *Who-What-When-Where-How-Why Made Easy.* Quadrangle, New York, 1972. A guide to the practical use of reference books. Tells how to find out what you want to know.

Moll, Edwin A., *Sell Yourself Big.* Topaz Books, Chicago 966. Dynamic, dramatic discusson on how to do your own public relations. Illustrated.

Murphey, Robert, *How and Where to Look It Up.* McGraw-Hill, New York, 1958. A guide to sources of information. Tells where to find out.

Musselman, Virginia W., *Money Raising Activities for Community Groups.* Association Press, New York, 1969. Complete instructions for putting on fairs and bazaars. Thirty pages on luncheons and dinners. A chapter on auctions and one on rummage sales. Brief descriptions of 27 other annual events.

Pleuther, Willard, *460 Secrets of Advertising Experts.* Thos. Nelson & Sons, New York, 1961. Twenty-three professionals each contribute 20 things they learned in 20 years in advertising.

Publicity Handbook: A Guide for Publicity Chairmen. Free upon request from the Sperry & Hutchinson Company, Consumer Relations, Cincinnati, Ohio. This booklet is 24 karat gold. Get it.

Samstag, Nicholas, *Persuasion for Profit*. University of Oklahoma Press, Oklahoma, 1957. Lots of original ideas on opportunities, strategies, and tactics of promotion.

Seeber, Edward, *Style Manual for Authors*. Indiana University Press, Bloomington, 1965. Small, compact, and complete desk book for writers.

Shepard, Harriett, and Meer, Lenore, *Posing for the Camera, a Professional Guide for the Creative Model, Director, and Photographer*. Hastings House, New York, 1960. Illustrated with drawings and diagrams. Cures the "I take terrible pictures" syndrome by showing what to do with hands, feet, faces, and bodies to produce flattering professional pictures.

Strunk, William, and White, E. B. *Elements of Style*, Macmillan, New York, 1959. Paperback. Highly recommended textbook on usage. Every writer should own this little book.

U. S. Government Printing Office, *Style Manual*. U. S. Government Printing Office, Washington, D. C., 1967. A no-nonsense book of rules on style, grammar, punctuation, composition, and proofreading. Notes that author's alterations cost the publisher money and cause delay.

Warren, Carl, *Modern News Reporting*. Harper & Bros., New York, 1959. An instructor in journalism at Northwestern University has produced a comprehensive book with lots of illustrations, subheads, and diagrams. Chapters on how to start the story, how to interview, and secrets of style.

Index